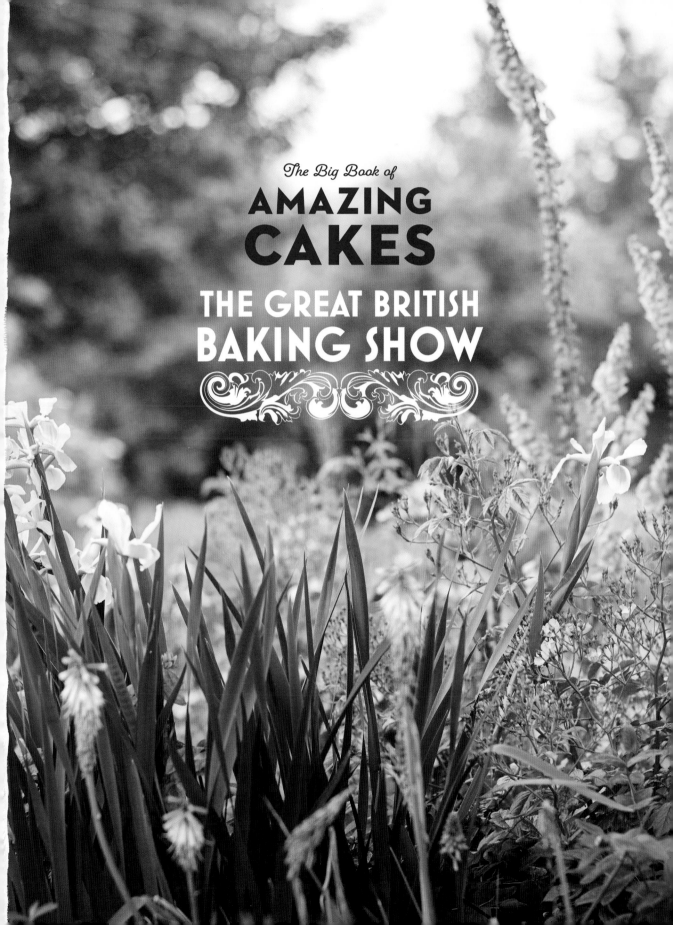

The Big Book of

AMAZING
CAKES

THE GREAT BRITISH
BAKING SHOW

CLARKSON POTTER / PUBLISHERS
NEW YORK

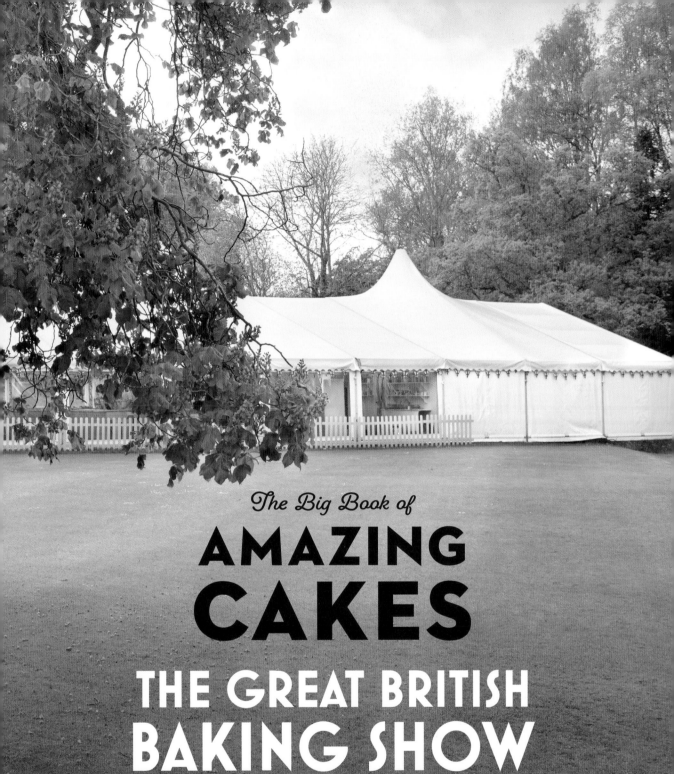

The Big Book of

AMAZING
CAKES

THE GREAT BRITISH
BAKING SHOW

CONTENTS

FOREWORD

A NOTE FROM PAUL

I can't believe it's been ten years! I've been so lucky to have been a part of *The Great British Baking Show* with Sandi, Noel, and Prue. We are constantly amazed and inspired by what the bakers come up with—every year brings new surprises—and the cakes made on the show always influence the baking community in a massive way.

This book is a celebration of cakes—some of the best bakers' recipes and technicals from this and past seasons, along with many more recipes for all levels of bakers. We want this to be the ultimate book for all cake bakers, with beautiful, delicious, and achievable cakes for everyone to make, reflecting the best of *Baking Show* cake-making.

Prue and I love coming up with the challenges—and the recipes in this book bring back so many memories from the seasons and the challenges we have set. Have a go at making the cakes in the comfort of your own home and become a star baker—and maybe even a winner—in your own kitchen.

A NOTE FROM PRUE

The first cake I ever baked was a Christmas cake at school. It took the whole term's lessons to make. It was iced with royal icing and I was immeasurably proud of it. But I hadn't put any glycerin into the icing and it set like concrete. My father broke my mother's favorite knife trying to cut it.

Not a good start. But since then I've baked hundreds of cakes; more so since being part of this show. *The Great British Baking Show* has been truly inspiring. Every week of this season we saw something completely different, wildly imaginative, or just utterly delicious.

It's a real pleasure to have such an extensive collection of cakes in this book, from the classics to the grand occasion cakes. Even the most complicated of them have step-by-step instructions so that anyone should be able to pick up the book and bake a great cake. We have recipes from the season and family favorites from this year's bakers, as well as irresistible recipes old and new that just can't be left out of a cake book.

I hope and trust and, indeed, believe that these recipes will have you reaching for a mixing bowl. And once started, you will keep going.

INTRODUCTION

This book provides the definitive celebration of cake. Featuring amazing cakes in all their guises (from well-loved classics to vegan bakes and from cupcakes to fondant fancies), we have brought together the ultimate *The Great British Baking Show* collection, aiming to excite and inspire, as well as—of course—to introduce you to our Season 10 bakers. As *Baking Show* celebrates its tenth birthday, we've also included a selection of the amazing cakes from the previous seasons, and you'll also find plenty of new cake recipes that will capture your attention.

Chapters on classic, chocolate, fruit & nut and free-from cakes each open with a perfect example of a cake in that category (the Victoria Sponge in Classics, the Ultimate Chocolate Cake in Chocolate, the Traditional Fruitcake in Fruit & Nut, and the Vegan Lemon Drizzle in Free-From). Each of these recipes is followed by a table that gives you recipe quantities for alternate sizes and shapes of that cake, so that you can adapt and experiment to create something that's just right for you. Then, every chapter features page after delicious page of other cake delights, each presented with clear, step-by-step instructions that leave nothing to chance.

An additional chapter, sitting at the very heart of the book, is a personal glimpse into the worlds of the Season 10 bakers, featuring their own family favorites and including some of the cakes that inspired them to start baking themselves.

Icons at the top of each recipe show how many people each cake serves, and hands-on times to give you a sense of how long you can expect to spend gathering your ingredients, and then mixing, and decorating your cake. The baking time is an instant guide to how long the baked elements of each cake will need in the oven (always follow the precise baking times given in the method).

Before you get started, read our guide to the chemistry of baking, which includes information on the role of each key ingredient, and how to use your oven to get the best results every time. And, because we want to inspire you not only to create the amazing cakes in the book but also to invent your own, information on the key methods of making cakes will help you to grow in confidence and experiment in your own kitchen. The storage information on page 20 will help you to keep your cake for longer should you have any left over, or if you are saving your bake for a particular day. Finally, throughout the book, key techniques (piping cupcakes, decorating with chocolate, and creating a showstopping naked effect) provide you with simple, step-by-step guidance on how to make the very most of your own amazing cakes.

On your marks, get set, bake!

THE CHEMISTRY OF CAKE-MAKING

Cake-making requires precision and a fundamental respect for the science that goes into every recipe. This might sound daunting, but actually it's the opposite: as long as you weigh your ingredients precisely and follow the method carefully, you should get the right result every time. Here are a few Baking Show insights into the chemistry within every cake.

THE INGREDIENTS

At its simplest a cake is a combination of flour, eggs, sugar, fat (in the form of butter, vegetable shortening, or oil), and perhaps a rising agent (such as baking powder or baking soda). It's a short list, but each ingredient does a specific job in the chemistry of cake-making, and the combination of ingredients gives you the taste, texture, and rise you want. That's why accurate weighing and measuring are so important.

Flour

Flour gives your cake structure. Wheat flour contains protein in varying amounts, which when mixed with liquid forms gluten. Stretchy and elastic, gluten provides the strength that holds a cake together. But you want exactly the right amount of gluten—too much and a cake will be tough; too little and it will be too tender. Most recipes stipulate to fold the flour gently into the creamed or whisked cake batter—this is to avoid overdeveloping the gluten in the flour.

From nuts and pulses to grains, flour can be made from many different core ingredients, but most traditional cakes require wheat-based all-purpose flour (which usually calls for the addition of a rising agent, such as baking powder) or self-rising flour (which already has rising agents in it). Sifting the flour is particularly important when making cakes, as it gets rid of any lumps and adds air.

Gluten-free baking

Gluten-free flour is made from rice, nuts, buckwheat, potatoes, chestnuts, oats, or chickpeas—or a combination of them. These flours don't naturally produce gluten, so gluten-free recipes usually use either xanthan gum or guar gum to help produce a cake-like texture, keeping the cake moist and stopping it from falling apart. Gluten-free flours labeled specifically for cake baking have gum already incorporated, but if you are making your own gluten-free mixture, add in the gum with the dry ingredients, as it is more difficult to combine once you have added the liquid. Making gluten-free cakes is not as straightforward as substituting gluten-free flour for wheat—the amount of liquid, the baking time, and the baking temperature may also change. As always, then, follow the recipe.

Sugar

Sugar gives a cake much more than just sweetness. It keeps a cake moist and, after baking, gives it its wonderful golden color. Like all the other ingredients, it also has a critical role to play in the production of air. Sugar both helps to create air bubbles during the creaming or whisking stage and interferes with the development of gluten in the flour, guaranteeing the finished cake a light, tender texture.

Different types of sugar and sweeteners have different effects on a cake. Most recipes will call for granulated sugar, especially if the cake uses the creaming method (see page 17), as the small crystals of granulated sugar enable more bubbles to form, increasing the lightness of a cake. Dark brown sugar will produce a richer color and flavor, but also a denser texture. Honey, molasses, and golden syrup—which caramelize as they cook—are often used in cakes made with the melting method (see page 19) and result in a dense, moist cake with less air, such as gingerbread.

Eggs

When you beat eggs together with fat and sugar, they create a light foam—bubbles of air attach themselves to the uneven edges of the sugar crystals and the layer of fat holds them in place. When cakes heat up in the oven, the air in the foam expands and the eggs solidify around the bubbles to keep them intact. This creates the final structure of the cake. Eggs also help to create that beautiful golden brown color of cakes.

Most recipes call for eggs at room temperature and to add them gradually to avoid the mixture curdling (although adding a little flour will fix the problem; see page 17).

Fat

In the form of butter, vegetable shortening, or oil, fat keeps cakes moist and adds flavor. But perhaps fat's most important job is to coat the flour molecules, protecting them from the egg or milk, which would cause more gluten to form and produce a heavier cake. Fat also traps air, creating lots of tiny air bubbles.

Preferences vary when it comes to which fat to use—some bakers argue that butter tastes better, while others say vegetable oil spread is best for creaming, as it tends to be softer and is better at trapping air during mixing. Either way, the fat needs to be at room temperature before use, because if it is too cold, it won't absorb much air. Cakes, such as carrot cake, made using the melting method (see page 19), which have a moist texture and dense crumb, often call for vegetable oils.

Rising agents

Also known as chemical leavening agents, rising agents, as their name suggests, help a cake to rise. The most common are baking powder and baking soda. These react with moisture in the cake mixture to create carbon dioxide, which fills and expands the air bubbles that were created during creaming or whisking. Always measure the amount of rising agent carefully, as too much can taint the flavor of a cake; and always mix baking soda with an acidic ingredient, such as yogurt, buttermilk, or cream of tartar, to activate it.

THE BAKING

It's not just the ingredients that require careful attention when baking cakes. The method and the equipment you use (and how you use it) are just as important, so here are a few general tips to help you. As always, follow the recipe carefully and all should be fine.

Baking pans

Size matters when it comes to baking pans, so always use the size, shape, and depth specified in the recipe. (Changing the size or shape of the pan will affect the baking time.)

Any style of pan is obviously going to do the job, but if you have a choice, a dull, light-colored pan is preferable to a shiny one (which will reflect heat) or a dark one (which will absorb too much heat and might over-bake your cake). Generally, a good-quality, durable pan will distribute the heat evenly.

Preparing your pan properly is also key. Do this before you start making your mixture, so that the pan is ready to use as soon as the mixture is ready.

Ovens

Get to know your oven because ovens vary in accuracy. If you can, use an oven thermometer.

Make sure you've heated the oven to the correct temperature before putting the cake inside. If you start baking the cake when the temperature is too low, your cake probably won't rise and may even have a sunken top. If the oven is too hot, your cake will cook too quickly on the outside, have a peaked top, and will probably burn.

The middle shelf of the oven is best for cake baking, to avoid burning the top of the cake. However, if you have a convection fan-assisted oven, where you position the cake shouldn't be an issue, as the fan will evenly distribute the heat. Never slam the door of your oven with the cake inside, as the vibration can burst the air bubbles in the sponge, causing the cake to sink—and try not to open the door at all during baking, as the resulting change in temperature can also make the cake sink.

Doneness

So, after all that, how do you know when your cake is ready to come out of the oven? As ovens can vary, this is a bit less scientific. Check the cake 5 to 10 minutes before the given baking time. Start by turning the light on in the oven, rather than opening the door, unless you really think your cake is ready. If your cake is looking brown on top and starting to shrink slightly from the edge of the pan, open the oven. A cake that's done should produce a lovely, cookie-like smell. If it's a whisked cake, touch the top gently with your finger—it should spring back; if it's a creamed cake, insert a skewer into the middle—it should come out clean. (If there's cake mixture on the skewer, you need to bake the cake for a little longer and test again.)

Cooling

When you take the cake out of the oven, most recipes suggest giving it from 5 to 10 minutes to cool in the pan before releasing and cooling it on a wire rack. Unless specified otherwise, if you leave the cake in the pan, it will continue to bake and may overcook.

METHODS OF MAKING CAKES

Watch a season of Baking Show and you'll learn pretty quickly that there are a few subtly different ways to make a cake. It's all about how you combine the various ingredients, and whether you mix the butter and sugar first or just add everything at once.

CREAMING METHOD

For a creamed cake, mix the softened butter (or the vegetable oil spread) with the sugar before adding the dry ingredients. Beat until the mixture becomes pale in color and has a light, creamy consistency. Some recipes suggest beating the butter (or spread) first on its own until pale and creamy, then adding the sugar gradually while continuing to beat. You can beat the butter and sugar with a wooden spoon, or use an electric hand mixer or a stand mixer, usually on medium speed. The length of time you'll need to beat obviously depends on the method you use, but it can range from 3 to 20 minutes for creaming by hand with a wooden spoon. This method adds lots of air to the mixture, which helps the cake to rise and gives it a light texture.

After creaming together the butter and sugar, beat the eggs in one at a time (or if the ingredients call for beaten eggs, add them little by little) to prevent the cake batter from curdling. The protein in the eggs stretches with the continued beating, holding the tiny air bubbles in place. Finally, fold in the flour gently to ensure that you keep as much air as possible in the mixture.

This method is used to make cakes such as the classic Victoria Sponge (see page 25) and the Blackberry Pound Cake (see page 182).

Creaming tips

» Make sure the butter or vegetable oil spread is at room temperature for easy creaming. People often pop it in the microwave to soften it—but be careful: if it's too soft, or is melting, the cake will not rise well.

» Granulated sugar is the best sugar to use for a creamed cake as it has small grains, unlike large-crystal sugar, and creates a pale and fluffy texture. Larger grains may result in a speckled appearance and crunchy texture after baking; while confectioners' sugar is too fine and powdery.

» If the cake mixture curdles when you add the eggs, add 1 tablespoonful of the flour (or flour mixture) with each addition of egg to help stabilize it. When the batter is smooth, fold in the remaining flour.

» When folding in the flour, use a large metal spoon and a gentle figure-eight movement until the flour is mixed in—this will keep in as much air as possible.

WHISKING METHOD

This method is usually used for lower-fat, lighter sponges, such as a roulades or Swiss rolls. Whisking the eggs and sugar replaces the need for a rising agent, such as baking powder or self-rising flour, to give the cake a light texture and good rise. Traditionally, you whisk the eggs and sugar together in a bowl set over a pan of gently simmering water until the mixture increases in volume by about four times and is thick enough to leave a ribbon trail when you lift the whisk. The mixture will also become pale and creamy.

Then you fold in the flour in batches, taking care not to knock the air out of the mixture. Sometimes, such as with a génoise sponge, you add melted butter, which makes a light cake with a soft sponge. Angel cake (see page 63), on the other hand, is traditionally butter- and egg-yolk-free and is a delicate cake with a slightly dry texture.

Some recipes using the whisking method call for separating the eggs. In that case, you whisk the egg yolks with the sugar until pale, thick and creamy. Then you whisk the egg whites separately until they reach stiff peaks, and then fold them in (alternately with the flour, if using). You'd use this method for a meringue cake, for example.

Whisking tips

» When whisking over a pan of water, do not allow the bowl to touch the water or the water to boil, as the mixture will become too hot and the eggs will start to scramble.

» Allow the cake batter to cool to room temperature before adding the flour.

» Bake the cake as soon as you've made it, as the whisked batter is unstable. It's particularly important with a whisked cake to avoid opening the oven until the cake is ready.

MELTING METHOD

This is one of the easiest methods for making cake as there's no beating or whisking involved to aerate the mixture. Instead, you melt the butter, usually with sugar, then add it to the eggs, followed by the dry ingredients, including all-purpose flour with a rising agent, such as baking powder. This method produces a cake with a dense, moist crumb and is used for gingerbread and some brownies and blondies.

Melting tips

» Let the melted butter or butter-sugar mixture cool to room temperature before adding the eggs and dry ingredients.

» Fold the sifted dry ingredients into the wet ingredients, working as quickly as possible.

ALL-IN-ONE CAKES

This method is exactly what it says it is, and couldn't be easier to make. You simply put all the ingredients in one bowl, mix them together with a wooden spoon or electric stand mixer and then bake in the oven. Vanilla, chocolate, or coffee sponge cakes suit this method.

All-in-one tips

» When you sift in the dry ingredients, raise the sieve as high as you can above the bowl to maximize the flour's contact with the air.

» Try not to overmix the cake batter—you want to keep in every air bubble to make sure the cake rises properly.

HOW TO STORE A CAKE

WRAP IT UP

Cakes that are covered with icing tend to stay moist because the coating provides a natural wrapping that helps to retain the moisture in the cake. If your cake is topped with buttercream, store it in a cake tin or airtight plastic container lined with parchment paper (in the fridge is best; see below). Note that strong flavors can taint a plastic container—a good wash to remove previous odors before using again is essential.

Undecorated sponges—whether whole or in slices—fare well wrapped in plastic wrap. Wrap tightly with no gaps to stop the cake from drying out. Cakes will keep at cool room temperature for 1 to 2 weeks.

Fruit cakes encased in marzipan and icing will last much longer than regular sponges (up to 1 month, or even longer if laced with alcohol), but in this case use only a cake tin or a box for storage, as plastic can make the cake sweat and go moldy.

KEEP IT COOL

Cakes with buttercream or ganache topping will last for 3 to 4 days in the fridge, stored in an airtight container. If the cake has custard, cream, cream cheese, or fresh fruit, it will last 1 to 2 days at most. Allow any cake you have refrigerated to come up to room temperature before you serve it. Finally, avoid refrigerating cakes with sugar paste, fondant, or food coloring, because the colors can bleed.

FREEZE IT

Undecorated sponges are perfect for freezing (freeze buttercream or icing separately, in an airtight container). Wrap the sponge well in plastic wrap, add a layer of foil if you like, and then place in an airtight plastic container or resealable bag—this will stop your cake from absorbing other flavors in the freezer. You can freeze basic sponges for about 4 months.

Allow your cakes to defrost completely before serving (it can take about 3 hours for a Victoria sponge to defrost at room temperature). If you've frozen the buttercream, defrost it, add a splash of milk to loosen it, and whip it to make it fluffy and spreadable. If you need to level your sponges before decorating, defrost them first.

AND FINALLY...

Even if you intend to eat your cake on the day, a few key tips will keep it at its best. Allow your cakes to cool completely on a wire rack before decorating—any residual steam or heat can cause icing to melt. While your cake is cooling and after decorating, keep the cake out of direct sunlight, which can dry out the sponge and discolor the icing.

If your kitchen is very warm, or if it's a hot summer day, even if you plan to eat your cake within hours of baking, store it in the fridge until you're ready, leaving just enough time for it to come up to room temperature before serving.

CHAPTER ONE

Classics

This is the standard Victoria sponge recipe for two 8-inch sponges to sandwich together, but it's easy to adapt for different shapes and sizes. Use the table on the following page to help you.

Victoria Sponge

FOR THE SPONGE
¾ cup plus 2 Tbsp unsalted
    butter, softened
1 cup granulated sugar
1 tsp vanilla extract
4 large eggs, beaten
1¾ cups self-rising flour, sifted
1 tsp baking powder
½ cup homemade or good-
    quality strawberry jam
confectioners' sugar, for
    dusting

FOR THE BUTTERCREAM
7 Tbsp unsalted butter,
    softened
1⅔ cups confectioners' sugar,
    sifted
½ tsp vanilla paste

YOU WILL NEED
8-inch round cake pans x 2,
    greased, then base-lined
    with parchment paper
large disposable piping bag
    (optional)

1 Heat the oven to 350°F.

2 Beat the butter, granulated sugar, and vanilla in the bowl of a stand mixer fitted with the paddle attachment, on medium speed for 5 to 6 minutes, until pale and creamy.

3 Add the eggs, a little at a time, beating well after each addition until well combined. If the mixture curdles, add 1 tablespoon of the flour and combine again.

4 In a separate bowl, use a fork to stir together the flour and baking powder. Then fold the dry ingredients into the wet ingredients, until just incorporated.

5 Divide the cake mixture equally between the two pans. Bake for 25 to 30 minutes, until golden and springy and a skewer inserted into the centers comes out clean. Cool the sponges in the pans for 5 minutes, then turn out onto a wire rack to cool completely.

6 Make the buttercream: Beat the butter, confectioners' sugar, and vanilla together in the bowl of a stand mixer fitted with the paddle attachment, on medium speed for 1 to 2 minutes, until fluffy.

7 To assemble, place one of the cooled sponges upside down on a cake plate or stand. Spread with the jam, then spread the buttercream over the top. Alternatively, fill the piping bag with the buttercream and snip a ½-inch hole in the end. Pipe the buttercream in little blobs around the outside edge of the sponge, then use an offset spatula to swirl it in toward the center to completely cover.

8 Place the second sponge on top. Press the sponges gently together, then dust with confectioners' sugar before serving.

SCALING QUANTITIES
VICTORIA SPONGE

Use this table to adjust your Victoria sponge mixture according to the size or shape of cake you want to make. The quantities for the 10-inch and 12-inch round cakes are for two 2-inch-deep cake pans. If you have only one pan, bake in two batches (half quantities for each batch), making one sponge, then repeating for a second.

	10-inch round, deep pan	12-inch round, deep pan	9 x 5-inch loaf pan	9 x 13-inch baking pan
For the sponge				
unsalted butter, softened	2 cups	3 cups plus 1 Tbsp	1 cup	1 cup plus 2 Tbsp
granulated sugar	2¼ cups	3½ cups	1 cup plus 2 Tbsp	1¼ cups
vanilla extract	1 Tbsp	2 Tbsp	1 tsp	1 tsp
large eggs, beaten	9	14	4	5
self-rising flour, sifted	4 cups	6 cups plus 3 Tbsp	2¼ cups	2¼ cups
baking powder	2 tsp	4 tsp	1 tsp	1 tsp
homemade/good-quality strawberry jam	¾ cup plus 3 Tbsp	1¾ cups plus 2 Tbsp	3 Tbsp	5 Tbsp
For the buttercream				
unsalted butter, softened	⅔ cup	¾ cup plus 2 Tbsp	⅓ cup	½ cup plus 1 Tbsp
confectioners' sugar	2 cups plus 6 Tbsp	3¼ cups	1¼ cups	2 cups
vanilla paste	1½ tsp	2 tsp	½ tsp	1 tsp
Baking time @ 350°F	40 to 45 mins	45 mins	45 to 50 mins	25 to 30 mins

Named to honor the union of Queen Victoria's granddaughter and Prince Louis Battenberg in 1884, Battenberg sponge has a checkered design that is iconic among classic cakes.

Battenberg

¾ cup unsalted butter, softened, plus extra for greasing
¾ cup plus 2 Tbsp granulated sugar
3 large eggs
1½ cups self-rising flour, sifted
½ tsp almond extract
pink food-coloring gel
¼ cup homemade or good-quality apricot jam, sieved
14 oz yellow marzipan
confectioners' sugar, for dusting

YOU WILL NEED
8-inch square, deep cake pan
2-in-1 parchment and foil
cake smoother (optional)

1 Using a double layer of 2-in-1 parchment and foil, fold a barrier to divide the cake pan in half, parchment side upward. Grease both the base and sides of the pan and the exposed parchment paper.

2 Heat the oven to 350°F.

3 Cream the butter and sugar together in the bowl of a stand mixer fitted with the paddle attachment, on medium speed for 3 to 5 minutes, until pale and creamy.

4 Add the eggs, one at a time, beating well after each addition. Add the flour and the almond extract and beat until smooth.

5 Spoon half the mixture into one side of the divided cake pan. Add a few drops of pink food coloring to the remaining mixture in the bowl and mix until you have an even color. Spoon the pink mixture into the other side of the cake pan.

6 Bake the cakes for 25 to 30 minutes, until a skewer inserted into the centers comes out clean. Cool in the pan for 10 minutes, then turn out onto a wire rack to cool completely.

7 Place the cooled sponges on a chopping board and, using a ruler, trim the sides of each cake to make straight edges. Cut each cake in half lengthwise to make two pink and two plain sponges. Trim the tops if they are different heights to create four identically shaped sponges.

8 Brush the apricot jam along the long sides of the cakes and join one plain and one pink slice together, lining up the short ends. Then place one pink and one plain sponge on top, sandwiching them with jam to create a checkered pattern. Brush apricot jam over all the long sides.

recipe continues

9 Roll out the marzipan on a work surface lightly dusted with confectioners' sugar to a rectangle measuring about 8 x 12 inches. Trim the edges to neaten.

10 Place the checkered cake onto the middle of the marzipan and wrap the marzipan around it, smoothing up the sides and around the corners so that the cake is tightly wrapped (you can use a cake smoother for this, if you have one).

11 To finish, turn the cake over so that the seam is on the underside and trim a thin slice of cake off each end to neaten. Using a sharp knife, score a crisscross pattern in the marzipan on the top of the cake.

Allowing a classic baked cheesecake to cool slowly in the oven will help prevent the top from cracking. This one also needs at least 2 hours in the fridge before serving, making it a good prepare-ahead dessert.

Baked Cheesecake

FOR THE CRUST
7 oz graham crackers
7 Tbsp unsalted butter, melted
finely grated zest of
    1 unwaxed lemon

FOR THE FILLING
4 cups full-fat cream cheese
1¼ cups plus 2 Tbsp
    granulated sugar
2 Tbsp all-purpose flour, sifted
a pinch of salt
1 tsp lemon juice
3 large eggs, plus 2 large yolks
1¼ cups sour cream
2 tsp vanilla extract
1⅔ cups raspberries, for
    decorating
confectioners' sugar, for
    dusting

YOU WILL NEED
9-inch springform cake pan,
    greased, then base-lined
    with parchment paper
large sheet of aluminum foil
    (enough to cover the base
    and reach above the sides of
    the pan)
large baking dish half filled
    with boiling water

1 Heat the oven to 400°F.

2 Make the crust: Place the graham crackers in a freezer bag and bash with a rolling pin to a crumb. Stir in the melted butter and 1 teaspoon of the lemon zest until combined (reserve the remaining lemon zest for the filling).

3 Tip the graham cracker mixture into the prepared pan and press down with a spoon. Bake for 10 minutes, then remove from the oven and set aside.

4 Make the filling: Beat the cream cheese in the bowl of a stand mixer fitted with the paddle attachment, on medium speed for 2 minutes, until smooth. Add the granulated sugar, flour, and salt and beat on low speed until incorporated.

5 With the mixer on medium speed, add the remaining lemon zest and the lemon juice. Then, add the whole eggs, one at a time, followed by the two yolks, mixing well after each addition. Stir in the sour cream and vanilla.

6 Pour the filling onto the crust and smooth into an even layer. Place the cheesecake on the large sheet of foil and gather up the foil around the sides of the pan (but not over the top).

7 Carefully place the cheesecake and foil into the baking dish with the boiling water and bake for 15 minutes. Then lower the oven to 225°F and bake for 50 minutes, until the filling is almost set.

8 Turn off the oven and let the cheesecake cool and set for 2 hours without opening the oven door. Then remove from the oven and refrigerate for 2 to 3 hours, before decorating with the raspberries and dusting with confectioners' sugar to serve.

MAKES **12** HANDS-ON **30** MINS BAKE **15** MINS

Once you get the hang of the two-tone frosting technique for these pretty fairy cakes, you can apply it to all manner of cakes—large and small.

Fairy Cakes

FOR THE SPONGE
7 Tbsp unsalted butter, softened
½ cup granulated sugar
1 tsp vanilla extract
2 large eggs, beaten
¾ cup plus 2 Tbsp self-rising flour, sifted

FOR THE BUTTERCREAM
¾ cup unsalted butter, softened
2¾ cups confectioners' sugar, sifted
1 tsp vanilla extract
pink food-coloring gel

YOU WILL NEED
12-cup muffin tin lined with 12 paper liners
large piping bag fitted with a large closed star nozzle

1 Heat the oven to 400°F.

2 Beat together the butter, granulated sugar, and vanilla in the bowl of a stand mixer fitted with the paddle attachment, on medium speed for 1 to 2 minutes, until pale and creamy.

3 With the machine still running, add the beaten eggs, little by little, until fully combined. Reduce the speed to low, and add the flour in two batches, beating until just combined after each addition.

4 Spoon equal amounts of the cake mixture into the paper liners and bake for 12 to 15 minutes, until golden, springy to the touch, and a skewer inserted into the centers comes out clean. Remove from the oven, place the tin on a wire rack and let the cakes cool completely.

5 While the cakes are cooling, make the buttercream: Beat the butter, confectioners' sugar, and vanilla in the bowl of a stand mixer fitted with the paddle attachment on low speed for 30 seconds, then increase the speed to medium and beat for 1 to 2 minutes, until pale and creamy.

6 Transfer half the buttercream to a bowl and color it your chosen shade of pink. Spoon the plain buttercream into the piping bag, keeping it to one side, then spoon the pink buttercream into the other side, trying not to let the buttercreams mix too much.

7 Starting at the center of each cupcake, pipe a spiral of buttercream working outward, to cover the whole cake, whipping the piping bag away quickly at the end of the spiral to avoid a tail of frosting.

HOW TO...
PIPE A BUTTERCREAM CUPCAKE

Buttercream is the classic cake topping and filling. This vanilla buttercream is ideal for piping. See page 38 for some cupcake piping techniques, too.

Vanilla buttercream frosting

**MAKES ENOUGH FOR
12 CUPCAKES (OR FILLING
FOR AN 8-INCH CAKE)**
¾ cup unsalted butter,
   softened
2¾ cups confectioners' sugar,
   sifted
1 tsp vanilla extract

Put the butter, sugar, and vanilla in the bowl of a stand mixer fitted with the paddle attachment. Beat on low speed for 30 seconds, until combined, then increase the speed to medium and beat for 3 minutes, until pale, smooth, and fluffy. (The longer you beat it the fluffier it will become.) You may need to stop the mixer to scrape down the bowl from time to time.

Alternatively, you can put the ingredients in a bowl and use an electric hand mixer, or you can beat the buttercream by hand with a wooden spoon—but obviously, it will take you longer to reach the desired consistency by hand.

Storage
The buttercream will keep for up to 3 days in an airtight container, stored in a cool place. It will also freeze well.

COLORING & FLAVORING BUTTERCREAM

To flavor or color buttercream, add your flavoring or coloring drop by tiny drop (a toothpick is good for this), stirring to combine after each addition, until you have just the flavor or color you want. Remember, you can always add more, but you can't take it away, so be patient.

As well as using store-bought flavorings, you can flavor buttercream with orange or lemon zest or juice, coffee, cocoa powder, liqueurs, or your favorite fruit purée.

Using a piping bag

Buttercream has to be just the right consistency for piping—too soft and it will not hold its shape; too firm and it will be difficult to achieve an even swirl. Ideally, it should be smooth and velvety with a whippy, fluffy consistency that is firm enough to retain the decoration, and is spreadable. If it is too thick, you could loosen it with a splash of milk; or if too thin, add a little more confectioners' sugar.

There are lots of different shapes and sizes of piping nozzles, giving a range of decorative effects. The most popular are plain, open star, and closed star.

For piping cupcakes with a nozzle, use a reuseable piping bag. To clean it after use, simply turn it inside out and pop it in the dishwasher, or wash it by hand in hot, soapy water.

1 Insert the nozzle into the pointed end of the piping bag, ensuring a cozy fit.

2 Fold the top of the piping bag over to make a collar—it will be much easier to fill this way. Spoon the buttercream into the bag so it is about half full, then twist the bag above the buttercream to direct the buttercream toward the nozzle, remove any air, and stop it from coming out of the bag as you pipe.

3 Use both hands. If you're right-handed, use your right hand to squeeze and your left hand to guide—vice versa if you're left-handed. You may find it easier to stand in order to gain height over your cake. Hold the piping bag perpendicular to the cake with the nozzle hovering just above, but not touching. Squeeze from the top using even pressure. See pages 40–41 for how to create specific effects.

CLASSIC SWIRL

You will need: large or small open star nozzle (depending on how tight you want your swirl)

Starting from the center of the cupcake, pipe a spiral outward to the edge. Then, in one smooth, circular motion, work your way inward to the center again, slightly overlapping as you go to give height. To finish, stop squeezing when you reach the center and draw up sharply to form a peak.

PEAKS

You will need: small or medium plain nozzle (depending on how large you want your peaks)

Starting from the center of the cupcake, gently squeeze the bag to form small peaks. Release the pressure and pull the bag away sharply at the end of each squeeze.

ROSE SWIRL

You will need: large closed star nozzle

Starting from the center of the cupcake, swirl the frosting in a smooth, circular motion, spiraling toward the edge, slightly overlapping as you go, until you have covered the cake. Pull away sharply at the end of the spiral.

GEMS

You will need: small, medium, or large open star nozzle (depending on how large you want your gems)

Starting from the center of the cupcake, gently squeeze the bag to form small peaks. Release the pressure and pull the bag away sharply at the end of each squeeze.

ROUNDED SWIRL

You will need: medium or large plain nozzle (depending on how tight you want your swirl)

Starting from the center of the cupcake, pipe a spiral outward to the edge, then, in one smooth, circular motion, work your way inward to the center again, slightly overlapping as you go to give height. To finish, stop squeezing when you reach the center and draw up sharply to form a peak.

FLOWERY SWIRL

You will need: medium or large petal nozzle (depending on how tall you want your petals)

Starting from the center of the cupcake, and with the narrowest part of the nozzle facing upward, move the piping bag in ever-increasing C shapes, overlapping each C with the next to form the petals around one another (you may find it easier to hold the cupcake in your free hand and turn it using your fingers as you go). Keep working outward in concentric circles until you have covered the cake.

Pipe a buttercream cupcake **41**

For a twist on this classic, add 1 teaspoon of ground cinnamon, cardamom, or pumpkin pie spice blend to the basic mixture.

Banana Bread

½ cup plus 1 Tbsp unsalted butter, softened
¾ cup plus 2 Tbsp light brown sugar
2 extra-large eggs, beaten
1 tsp vanilla extract
2 cups all-purpose flour
1 tsp baking soda
½ tsp salt
3 large or 4 medium very ripe bananas, well mashed
3 Tbsp sour cream

YOU WILL NEED
9 x 5-inch loaf pan, greased

1 Heat the oven to 350°F.

2 Beat the butter and sugar together in the bowl of a stand mixer fitted with the paddle attachment, on medium speed for 3 to 4 minutes, until pale and creamy.

3 Add the eggs, a little at a time, beating well after each addition, until fully combined, then add the vanilla.

4 Sift the flour, baking soda, and salt into a bowl. Add one third of the flour mixture, one third of the mashed banana, and 1 tablespoon of the sour cream to the creamed butter and sugar mixture and gently beat together. Repeat with another third of flour, banana, and sour cream, then finally the remaining third of each.

5 Spoon the mixture into the prepared loaf pan and bake for 1 hour (don't be tempted to open the oven door), until a skewer inserted into the center comes out clean.

6 Remove the loaf from the oven and allow it to cool in the pan for 15 minutes, then turn it out onto a wire rack to cool completely.

You'll need a cake-decorating turntable to create the spiral effect on the top of this cake, but don't worry if you don't have one—the decoration of real carrots is just as effective without a spiral.

Carrot Cake

FOR THE SPONGE
1½ cups plus 1 Tbsp light
     muscovado sugar
1¼ cups sunflower oil
6 large eggs, beaten
2 cups grated carrots
1¼ cups golden raisins
finely grated zest of
     1 unwaxed orange
2⅔ cups self-rising flour
1½ tsp baking soda
2 tsp pumpkin pie spice blend

FOR THE FROSTING
¾ cup plus 2 Tbsp unsalted
     butter, softened
3¼ cups confectioners' sugar,
     sifted
finely grated zest of
     1 unwaxed orange
1 tsp vanilla extract
¾ cup full-fat cream cheese,
     at room temperature

FOR THE DECORATION
2 Tbsp chopped hazelnuts
1 tsp cocoa powder
a few small carrots, green tops
     intact, washed and trimmed

YOU WILL NEED
8-inch round cake pans x 3,
     greased, then lined
     (base and sides)
     with parchment paper
cake-decorating
     turntable (optional)
large offset spatula (optional)

1 Heat the oven to 400°F.

2 Combine the sugar and oil in a large bowl and mix until the sugar has dissolved. Whisk in the eggs, then add the carrot, golden raisins, and orange zest and stir to combine.

3 Sift the flour, baking soda, and pumpkin pie spice together into a bowl, then fold the dry mixture into the wet mixture until no streaks of flour remain. Divide the mixture equally among the three prepared pans.

4 Bake the sponges for 30 to 35 minutes, until springy to the touch and a skewer inserted into the centers comes out clean. Cool in the pans for 5 minutes, then turn out onto a wire rack to cool completely.

5 Make the frosting: Beat the butter, confectioners' sugar, orange zest, and vanilla in the bowl of a stand mixer fitted with the paddle attachment, on medium speed for 1 to 2 minutes, until fluffy. Add the cream cheese and beat for 20 to 30 seconds more, until smooth and combined.

6 Level the cooled cakes, then place the first layer on a cake plate, and then on a turntable, if using. Spread one quarter of the buttercream over the top of the cake. Top with a second cake, and cover with another quarter of the buttercream. Finish with the final cake on top.

7 Hold the top of the cake firmly with one hand. Using an offset spatula, if you have one, push any excess frosting into the gaps between the layers.

8 Add half the remaining buttercream to the top of the cake and spread it out and down the sides to apply a crumb coat.

recipe continues

9 To create the naked effect on the side of the cake, gently smooth the spatula around the side to leave only a thin layer of buttercream that shows some of the dark sponge peeping through.

10 Top the cake with the remaining buttercream, using the spatula to spread it thickly all the way to the edges.

11 If you're using a turntable, to create the swirl effect, dip the end of the spatula into the buttercream in the center of the sponge, then spin the turntable while drawing the spatula outward, using a little pressure to create the spiral. Neaten the frosting around the top edge of the cake.

12 To decorate, in a bowl, combine the nuts and cocoa to create "soil." Crumble this over the cake as a patch for the sprouting carrots. Trim the pointed ends off the carrots and press the cut ends down into the patch of "soil," as if they are coming out of the cake.

We love the summery pink and yellow colors of these classic fondant fancies, but feel free to personalize them using your own favorite icing colors, if you prefer.

Fondant Fancies

FOR THE SPONGE
1 cup unsalted butter, softened
1 cup plus 2 Tbsp granulated
     sugar
4 large eggs
2 cups self-rising flour, sifted
finely grated zest of
     1 unwaxed lemon

FOR THE BUTTERCREAM
⅔ cup unsalted butter, softened
1⅔ cups confectioners' sugar,
     sifted
½ tsp vanilla extract

FOR THE MARZIPAN TOPPING
7 oz plain marzipan
3 Tbsp homemade or good-
     quality apricot jam, sieved

FOR THE ICING
& DECORATION
2 lb 4 oz ready-to-roll white
     fondant icing
yellow food-coloring gel
pink food-coloring gel
¾ cup confectioners' sugar,
     sifted
juice of ½ lemon
3½ oz 54% dark chocolate,
     broken into small pieces

YOU WILL NEED
8-inch square, deep cake pan,
     greased, then base-lined
     with parchment paper
medium piping bag fitted
     with a small plain nozzle
2 small piping bags, each fitted
     with a small writing nozzle

1 Heat the oven to 325°F.

2 For the sponge, beat the butter, sugar, eggs, flour, and lemon zest in the bowl of a stand mixer fitted with the paddle attachment, on medium speed for 2 minutes, until smooth. Tip the mixture into the prepared pan and tap lightly to level out. Bake for 35 to 40 minutes, or until a skewer inserted into the center comes out clean. Let cool in the pan for 10 minutes, then turn out onto a wire rack to cool completely. Chill the sponge in the refrigerator for 30 minutes.

3 For the buttercream, beat the butter, sugar, and vanilla together in a bowl until pale and fluffy. Place a scant ½ cup of the buttercream in the medium piping bag and refrigerate to firm up slightly. Reserve the remaining buttercream in the bowl.

4 Roll out the marzipan on a surface lightly dusted with confectioners' sugar to an 8-inch square. Remove the chilled cake from the fridge and brush the top with the apricot jam, then place the marzipan on top.

5 Cut the cake into 16 equal squares (each about 1¾ inches square). Using the buttercream in the bowl, cover the four sides of each square with buttercream (don't spread it over the marzipan top or the base). Then, using the buttercream in the piping bag, pipe a blob in the center of the marzipan on top of each square. Let the cakes set in the fridge for 20 minutes.

6 For the icing and decoration, cut the fondant icing into small cubes. Place the cubes in the bowl of a stand mixer fitted with the paddle attachment. Mix the fondant on low speed until it starts to break down, adding a splash of water if it's too hard. Very slowly add ½ cup plus 2 tablespoons of water until the fondant becomes smooth and pourable.

recipe continues

7 Divide the pourable fondant into two bowls. Color one bowl pale yellow and the other bowl pale pink. Be careful not to add too much coloring at once—you can always add more if you want the color a little darker.

8 Tip the confectioners' sugar into a bowl and add enough lemon juice to form smooth icing of dropping consistency (you may not need all the juice). Spoon the mixture into one of the piping bags fitted with a writing nozzle.

9 Melt the chocolate in a heatproof bowl set over a pan of gently simmering water, stirring occasionally. Once melted, pour the chocolate into the other piping bag fitted with a writing nozzle.

10 Take the cakes out of the fridge and place them on a wire rack set over a rimmed baking sheet (to catch the icing). Pour the yellow fondant over eight of the cakes and the pink fondant over the remaining eight cakes.

11 Let the fondant set for 5 to 10 minutes at room temperature, then using the piping bags, pipe the melted chocolate diagonally backward and forward over the yellow cakes and the white icing over the pink cakes. Let set for 2 to 3 hours on the wire rack before serving.

Drizzle while the cake is warm for the perfect soak.

Lemon Drizzle Traybake

FOR THE SPONGE
1 cup unsalted butter,
    diced and softened
1 cup plus 2 Tbsp granulated
    sugar
2½ cups self-rising flour, sifted
2 tsp baking powder
4 extra-large eggs
3 Tbsp whole milk
zest of 3 large or 4 medium
    unwaxed lemons

FOR THE DRIZZLE
juice of 3 large or
    4 medium lemons
¾ cup granulated sugar

TO DECORATE
3 Tbsp large-crystal sugar

YOU WILL NEED
9 x 13-inch baking pan,
    greased, then lined
    (base and sides)
    with parchment paper

1 Heat the oven to 325°F.

2 Beat together all the sponge ingredients in the bowl of a stand mixer fitted with the paddle attachment, on medium speed for 2 minutes, until smooth.

3 Transfer the mixture to the prepared pan and smooth the top. Bake for 35 to 40 minutes, until springy to the touch and a skewer inserted into the center comes out clean. Set aside to cool just a little while you quickly make the drizzle.

4 Stir together the lemon juice and sugar. Using a toothpick or skewer, poke holes all over the sponge and spoon the drizzle over. Let the sponge cool completely in the pan.

5 Sprinkle the traybake with the large-crystal sugar, then remove the sponge from the pan and cut into 24 squares.

This is a quick-and-easy classic cherry sponge cake given a little extra texture from the addition of ground almonds. Dusting the cherries with flour helps prevent them from sinking to the bottom of the cake.

Cherry Cake

7 oz maraschino or glacé
   cherries, quartered and
   rinsed
2 cups self-rising flour, sifted
¾ cup unsalted butter, softened
¾ cup plus 2 Tbsp granulated
   sugar
finely grated zest of
   1 unwaxed lemon
½ cup ground almonds
3 extra-large eggs

TO DECORATE
1 cup plus 6 Tbsp
   confectioners' sugar, sifted
juice of 1 lemon
3 Tbsp sliced almonds, toasted
5 maraschino or glacé cherries,
   quartered

YOU WILL NEED
9-inch savarin mold
   or Bundt pan, greased

1 Heat the oven to 350°F.

2 Dry the rinsed cherries thoroughly on paper towels and toss them in 2 tablespoons of the flour.

3 Put all the remaining sponge ingredients into a large bowl and beat well for 2 minutes to mix thoroughly. Lightly fold in the cherries until evenly distributed, then transfer the mixture to the prepared pan.

4 Bake for 35 to 40 minutes, until well risen, golden brown, and a skewer inserted into the cake comes out clean. Let cool in the pan for 10 minutes, then turn out onto a wire rack to cool completely.

5 For the decoration, mix the confectioners' sugar with the lemon juice to a thick paste. Drizzle the paste over the back of a spoon onto the cooled cake, then sprinkle the toasted almonds and quartered cherries over the top.

Adding the hot coffee to the sponge and frosting at the creaming stage helps to dissolve the sugar and lighten the mixture in this classic elevenses treat.

Coffee & Walnut Cake

FOR THE SPONGE
¾ cup plus 2 Tbsp unsalted
   butter, softened
1 cup granulated sugar
1 tsp vanilla extract
2 Tbsp instant espresso
2 to 3 Tbsp boiling water
4 large eggs, beaten
1¾ cups self-rising, sifted
1 tsp baking powder
¾ cup chopped walnuts,
   plus 7 walnut halves
   to decorate

FOR THE BUTTERCREAM
1 cup unsalted butter, softened
3⅔ cups confectioners' sugar,
   sifted
2 Tbsp instant espresso
2 Tbsp boiling water

YOU WILL NEED
8-inch round cake pans x 2,
   greased, then lined
   (base and sides)
   with parchment paper
large piping bag fitted with
   a large closed star nozzle

1 Heat the oven to 400°F.

2 Beat the butter, sugar, and vanilla together in the bowl of a stand mixer fitted with the paddle attachment, on medium speed for 1 to 2 minutes, until pale and creamy.

3 Dissolve the espresso powder in the boiling water, then add this to the creamed butter and beat on medium speed for 1 minute, until fluffy. Add the eggs, a little at a time, beating well after each addition.

4 With the mixer on low speed, add the flour and baking powder, mixing until just combined. Add the chopped walnuts and mix slowly for a few seconds, until evenly distributed.

5 Divide the mixture equally between the two pans and bake for 25 to 30 minutes, until a skewer inserted into the centers comes out clean. Let cool in the pans for 5 minutes, then turn out onto a wire rack to cool completely.

6 Make the buttercream: Beat the butter and sugar in the bowl of a stand mixer fitted with the paddle attachment, on medium speed for 1 minute. Dissolve the espresso powder in the boiling water, then with the mixer on low, add it to the bowl. Increase the speed to medium and cream for 1 to 2 minutes, until fluffy.

7 To assemble, place one sponge top-side downward onto a cake plate and spread with one third of the buttercream. Top with the second sponge, and use another third of the buttercream to cover.

8 Spoon the remaining buttercream into the piping bag fitted with the star nozzle. Pipe six swirls of buttercream around the top edge of the cake and one swirl in the center. Top each swirl with a walnut half.

Cakes don't get much simpler than this one. Cool it in the pan to allow the sponge to soak up all the gooey syrup. For an alternative, try replacing the vanilla with 1 tablespoon of ground ginger.

Pineapple Upside-Down Cake

8 canned pineapple rings
   in natural juice, drained
½ cup plus 1 Tbsp golden
   syrup or light corn syrup
7 maraschino or glacé cherries,
   halved
¾ cup plus 2 Tbsp unsalted
   butter
1 cup granulated sugar
1¾ cups self-rising, sifted
¾ tsp baking powder
3 extra-large eggs
5 Tbsp whole milk
1½ tsp vanilla extract

YOU WILL NEED
8-inch round cake pan,
   greased, then base-lined
   with parchment paper

1 Heat the oven to 350°F. Halve six of the drained pineapple rings and quarter the remaining two. Set aside.

2 Pour the golden syrup or light corn syrup into the prepared pan, tilting the pan to evenly spread the syrup. Arrange the pineapple halves in a circle around the edge of the pan and arrange the pineapple quarters in the middle. Place a cherry in the middle of each pineapple half and one cherry in the middle.

3 Place the butter, sugar, flour, and baking powder in the bowl of a food processor. Lightly beat the eggs, milk, and vanilla extract together in a pitcher, then add the mixture to the processor bowl. Blitz for 1 minute, until thoroughly blended.

4 Spoon the mixture into the pan and level out with an offset spatula. Bake for 35 to 45 minutes, until golden and a skewer inserted into the center comes out clean. Let the cake cool in the pan for at least 15 minutes, then invert onto a serving plate and cut into slices.

Parkin is a sticky cake flavored with syrupy molasses, oats, and ginger, traditionally enjoyed on Bonfire Night in the north of England. Like a fine wine, parkin improves with age, so bake it up to a week before you want to eat it.

Parkin

1 extra-large egg, beaten
¼ cup whole milk
1 cup plus 2 Tbsp rolled oats
¾ cup plus 2 Tbsp unsalted butter
5 Tbsp molasses
1 Tbsp golden syrup or light corn syrup
¼ cup dark brown sugar
2¼ cups self-rising flour, sifted
1 Tbsp ground ginger
1 tsp pumpkin pie spice blend

YOU WILL NEED
8-inch square cake pan, greased, then lined (base and sides) with parchment paper

1 Heat the oven to 325°F.

2 Beat the egg and milk together in a small bowl.

3 Using a food processor, blitz the oats to a coarse powder.

4 Place the butter in a large pot with the molasses, golden syrup or light corn syrup, and sugar. Melt everything together over low heat, stirring occasionally.

5 Remove the pot from the heat and stir in the ground oats, flour, ginger, and pumpkin pie spice. Add the egg and milk mixture and stir until well combined.

6 Pour the mixture into the prepared pan and bake for 50 minutes to 1 hour, until the sponge is firm to the touch but not dry. Let cool in the pan until completely cold, then wrap it (still in the pan) in parchment paper and foil. Store for 1 week, then turn out and cut into 16 squares. Eat within 2 weeks.

This is Prue's take on the retro English angel cake. The pretty decoration is super easy: a toothpick and stripes of pink icing are all you need.

Angel Cake Slices

FOR THE GÉNOISE
¼ cup unsalted butter,
  melted and cooled,
  plus extra for greasing
4 extra-large eggs, at room
  temperature
½ cup plus 2 Tbsp granulated
  sugar
1 cup all-purpose flour, sifted
½ tsp vanilla extract
½ tsp natural raspberry
  flavoring
pink food-coloring gel
finely grated zest of
  1 small unwaxed lemon
yellow food-coloring gel

**FOR THE ITALIAN MERINGUE
BUTTERCREAM**
½ cup granulated sugar
1 extra-large egg white
6 Tbsp unsalted butter,
  softened

FOR THE FONDANT ICING
2 cups fondant sugar or
  confectioners' sugar
pink food-coloring gel

YOU WILL NEED
2-in-1 parchment and foil cut
  to a 20 x 8-inch rectangle
9 x 13-inch baking pan
candy thermometer
small piping bag fitted with
  a medium writing nozzle

1 For the génoise, fold the foiled parchment to divide the baking pan into three even sections with the parchment side facing upward, and grease with melted butter. Heat the oven to 375°F.

2 Tip the eggs and sugar into a bowl set over a pan of gently simmering water. Gently whisk until the sugar has dissolved and the mixture reaches 109°F on a candy thermometer.

3 Weigh the mixture in the bowl of a stand mixer, then record the weight. Attach the bowl to the mixer and, using the whisk attachment, whisk the mixture until it is thick and mousse-like, and leaves a ribbon trail when you lift the whisk.

4 Meanwhile, divide the flour evenly among three small bowls. Do the same for the butter. Stir the vanilla into one bowl of butter. Stir the raspberry flavoring and a small drop of pink food coloring into the second bowl of butter, and the lemon zest and a small drop of yellow food coloring into the third.

5 Divide the whisked egg mixture into three bowls. Working with one bowl of egg mixture, flour, and butter at a time, sift the flour over the egg mixture and gently fold in. Add the butter and fold—work quickly to prevent the mixture from collapsing.

6 Repeat Step 5 with the remaining bowls of egg mixture, flour, and butter to create three mixtures—vanilla, raspberry, and lemon. Pour each into a section of the cake pan and bake for 12 to 15 minutes, until the tops spring back when pressed. Cool a little in the pan, then transfer to a wire rack to cool completely.

recipe continues

7 For the Italian meringue buttercream, melt the sugar in 3 tablespoons of water very gently in a pot over low heat. Meanwhile, whisk the egg white in the clean bowl of a stand mixer fitted with a whisk, to soft peaks. Once the sugar has completely dissolved, increase the heat to a rapid boil until the syrup reaches 250°F on a candy thermometer.

8 Remove the pot from the heat. With the mixer at full speed, slowly pour the hot syrup onto the egg whites in a thin stream. Continue whisking until the meringue is very thick and glossy and has cooled to room temperature.

9 Gradually add the butter, whisking after each addition until the buttercream is smooth and thick. Chill until firm.

10 To assemble, trim the sponges so they are identical in size and height. Spread half the buttercream over the vanilla sponge and top with the raspberry sponge. Spread the other half of the buttercream over the raspberry sponge and top with the lemon sponge (you might not need all the buttercream).

11 For the fondant icing, sift the icing sugar into a bowl and add 1½ to 2 tablespoons of water to mix to a stiff, dropping consistency. Spoon one quarter of the icing into a small bowl and color it pink. Spoon the pink icing into the piping bag fitted with a writing nozzle.

12 Spread the white fondant icing over the top (not the sides) of the lemon sponge. Pipe fine lines of icing across the width of the cake, spacing them ½ inch apart. Using a toothpick, gently drag the icing lines in opposite directions through the white fondant to feather. Cut the cake into six even slices and serve.

Madeira cake is not named after the islands, but for the fortified Portuguese wine that comes from them. The association is fitting because, like the cake, Madeira wine is baked in an oven.

Madeira Cake

FOR THE SPONGE
⅔ cup unsalted butter, softened
¾ cup granulated sugar
4 large eggs, beaten
1¾ cups self-rising flour, sifted
a pinch of salt
finely grated zest of
    2 unwaxed oranges
finely grated zest of
    1 large unwaxed lemon

FOR THE CANDIED PEEL
rind of 1 unwaxed orange,
    cut into matchsticks
rind of 1 unwaxed lemon,
    cut into matchsticks
6 Tbsp granulated sugar

FOR THE ICING
1¼ cups confectioners' sugar,
    sifted
juice of ½ to 1 lemon

YOU WILL NEED
9 x 5-inch loaf pan, greased,
    then dusted with flour

1 Heat the oven to 350°F.

2 Beat the butter and sugar in the bowl of a stand mixer fitted with the paddle attachment, on medium speed for 5 minutes, until pale and creamy.

3 Add the eggs, a little at a time, beating well after each addition. Add the flour, salt, and orange and lemon zests and beat until smooth.

4 Spoon the mixture into the prepared pan and level with an offset spatula. Bake for 50 to 55 minutes, until a skewer inserted into the center comes out clean. Cool in the pan for 15 minutes, then transfer to a wire rack to cool completely.

5 Meanwhile, make the candied peel: Bring a large pot of water to a boil, add the matchsticks of orange and lemon peel. Boil for 15 seconds, then drain through a sieve. Return the peel to the pot and add the sugar and 5 tablespoons of water. Bring to a boil and boil for 8 to 10 minutes, until the liquid is syrupy. Remove the peel from the pot and place it on a wire rack to cool.

6 For the icing, mix the confectioners' sugar and lemon juice together to form a thick paste (you may not need all the juice).

7 Once the cake is cool, pour the icing over the top of the cake and scatter the candied peel on top.

Baked in just 10 minutes, this classic is delicious rolled with homemade jam or lemon curd, and sublime with whipped cream, too. As it is a fatless sponge, it doesn't store particularly well, so eat it on the day you make it.

Swiss Roll

4 large eggs, at room temperature

½ cup granulated sugar, plus extra for sprinkling

¾ cup plus 1 Tbsp all-purpose flour

a pinch of salt

½ cup homemade or good-quality fruit jam or lemon curd

1 cup heavy cream, whipped to soft peaks

YOU WILL NEED

9 x 13-inch baking pan, greased, then lined with parchment paper

14-inch-long sheet of parchment paper

1 Heat the oven to 425°F.

2 Whisk the eggs and sugar in the bowl of a stand mixer fitted with the whisk attachment on high speed, until the mixture is thick and mousse-like, and leaves a ribbon trail when you lift the whisk.

3 Sift the flour and salt onto a sheet of parchment paper, then sift half of it over the egg mixture. Fold it in with a metal spoon, then sift in the remaining flour and salt and fold until the mixture is smooth and streak-free. Gently scrape down the sides of the bowl and check the bottom of the mixture for any pockets of flour—incorporate them if you find them.

4 Pour the mixture into the prepared pan and gently tip the pan so that the mixture flows into the corners and is level. Bake for 9 to 10 minutes, until golden brown and springy to the touch.

5 Lay the sheet of parchment paper on the work surface and sprinkle with sugar. As soon as you take the sponge out of the oven turn it out onto the sugar-coated paper—lift off the pan and peel away the parchment paper that had lined the pan.

6 Turn the sponge so that one of the short ends is closest to you. Using a sharp knife, score a cut ¾ inch in from the short end—this will help the roll. Starting from that end, gently roll up the Swiss roll with the sheet of paper rolled inside. Place the roll on a wire rack and let cool completely.

7 To assemble, gently unroll the roll and trim off the edges with a sharp knife. Spread with jam or lemon curd, leaving a ¾-inch border around the edge. Cover the jam with a layer of whipped cream, keeping the ¾-inch border.

8 Starting again at the scored end of the roll, gently roll up, this time without the parchment paper. Turn the roll seam-side down and sprinkle with sugar before serving.

SERVES	HANDS-ON	BAKE
12	1 HOUR	25 MINS

This cheery American classic is traditionally baked for Christmas and Valentine's Day—but really it suits any occasion. If you wish, you could leave the sides of the cake naked or semi-naked.

Red Velvet Cake

FOR THE SPONGE
1⅔ cups unsalted butter, softened
1½ cups plus 2 Tbsp granulated sugar
4 large eggs, beaten
3 Tbsp cocoa powder
2 tsp vanilla extract
2 Tbsp red food-coloring paste
7 Tbsp hot water
1½ cups buttermilk
1 tsp salt
4 cups self-rising flour, sifted
1½ tsp white vinegar
1½ tsp baking soda

FOR THE BUTTERCREAM
1 cup plus 2 Tbsp unsalted butter, softened
2 tsp vanilla extract
4 cups confectioners' sugar, sifted
¾ cup plus 2 Tbsp full-fat cream cheese, at room temperature

YOU WILL NEED
8-inch round cake pans x 3, greased then lined (base and sides) with parchment paper

1 Heat the oven to 400°F.

2 Beat the butter and sugar in the bowl of a stand mixer fitted with the paddle attachment, on medium speed for 2 to 3 minutes, until pale and creamy. Add the eggs, a little at a time, beating well after each addition until combined.

3 In a small bowl, mix the cocoa powder, vanilla, red food coloring, and hot water together to form a paste. Add this to the cake mixture and mix well until combined.

4 Combine the buttermilk and salt in a pitcher. Add one third to the bowl with the cake mixture, then add one third of the flour. Alternate buttermilk and flour, until everything is combined.

5 In a small bowl, mix the vinegar and baking soda together and add to the cake mixture. Beat until smooth.

6 Divide the mixture equally among the prepared pans and bake for 20 to 25 minutes, until springy to the touch and a skewer inserted into the centers comes out clean. Cool in the pans for 5 minutes, then turn out onto a wire rack to cool completely.

7 To make the buttercream, beat the butter and vanilla in the bowl of a stand mixer fitted with the paddle attachment, on high speed for about 1 minute, until smooth and fluffy.

8 Add the confectioners' sugar, one quarter at a time, beating after each addition slowly at first, then on high speed for about 1 minute. With the mixer on low, add the cream cheese and beat briefly, until smooth.

recipe continues

9 To assemble, level the sponges, keeping any trimmings for decoration. Smear a little buttercream onto a cake plate and top with the first sponge.

10 Spread one quarter of the buttercream on top, overhanging the edge a little, then top with a second sponge. Spread another quarter of the buttercream—again, leave an overhang. Top with the remaining sponge.

11 With an offset spatula, spread the overhanging buttercream all around the side of the cake, to seal and neaten.

12 Next, using one third of the remaining buttercream, spread a thin, even layer over the top of the cake.

13 Clean the spatula and smooth off any excess buttercream to create a crumb coat. Chill the cake in the refrigerator for at least 30 minutes to firm up, then add a second, slightly thicker coat using the remaining buttercream.

14 To decorate the cake, crumble the reserved trimmings and sprinkle them neatly around the edge of the top of the cake.

CHAPTER TWO

Chocolate

The secret to a great chocolate cake is not to overbake it—when you insert the skewer it's okay if it comes out a little sticky (but not wet). A gooey cake will last you a few days without going dry.

Ultimate Chocolate Cake

FOR THE SPONGE
10 oz 70% dark chocolate, broken into pieces
1¼ cups unsalted butter, softened
1¾ cups light muscovado sugar
2 tsp vanilla extrtact
4 large eggs, plus 4 large egg yolks, beaten together
¾ cup plus 2 Tbsp sour cream
1 tsp baking powder
⅔ cup cocoa powder, sifted
2¼ cups self-rising flour, sifted

FOR THE BUTTERCREAM
¾ cup plus 2 Tbsp dark chocolate chips
1 cup plus 2 Tbsp unsalted butter, softened
4 cups confectioners' sugar, sifted
⅓ cup sour cream

YOU WILL NEED
8-inch springform pans x 2, greased, then lined (base and sides) with parchment paper
large piping bag fitted with a medium petal nozzle

1 Heat the oven to 350°F.

2 Make the sponge: Melt the chocolate in a bowl set over a pot of simmering water. Remove from the heat and let cool.

3 Beat the butter, sugar, and vanilla in the bowl of a stand mixer fitted with the paddle attachment, on medium speed for about 5 minutes, until pale and creamy. Reduce the speed to low and add the eggs, a little at a time, beating well after each addition. If the mixture begins to curdle, add 1 tablespoon of the flour and mix again.

4 With the mixer on low speed, pour in the cooled, melted chocolate, then the sour cream. Mix to combine, then add the baking powder, cocoa powder, and flour, one third at a time, mixing after each addition until just combined.

5 Divide the mixture equally between the prepared pans. Bake for 35 to 45 minutes, until a skewer inserted into the centers comes out sticky. Put the pans on a wire rack and let cool.

6 Make the buttercream: Melt the chocolate chips in a bowl set over a pot of simmering water. Remove from the heat and let cool.

7 Beat the butter and confectioners' sugar in the bowl of a stand mixer fitted with the paddle attachment, on medium speed for 3 to 5 minutes, until pale and creamy, then add the cooled chocolate and sour cream. Beat for 1 minute, until smooth.

8 Once the cakes are cool, cut each cake in half horizontally. Place one sponge, top-side down, on a plate. Transfer one third of the buttercream to the piping bag and set aside. Spread one third of the remaining buttercream over the top of the cake, then top with the next sponge. Repeat twice more and top with the final sponge. Pipe buttercream petals from the center outward, to cover the cake.

SCALING QUANTITIES
ULTIMATE CHOCOLATE CAKE

Use this table to adjust your chocolate cake mixture according to the size or shape of cake you want to make. The quantities for the 10-inch and 12-inch round cakes are for two 2-inch-deep cake pans. If you have only one pan, bake in two batches (half quantities for each batch), making one sponge, then repeating for a second. The buttercream quantities will fill and top the round cakes, and top the loaf and the 9 x 13-inch cake.

	10-inch round, deep cake pan	12-inch round, deep cake pan	9 x 5-inch loaf pan	9 x 13-inch baking pan
For the chocolate sponge				
70% dark chocolate, broken into pieces	15 oz	1 lb 6 oz	6 oz	10 oz
unsalted butter, softened	1¾ cups plus 2 Tbsp	2¾ cups	¾ cup	1¼ cups
light muscovado sugar	2⅔ cups	3¾ cups plus 1 Tbsp	1 cup plus 1 Tbsp	1¾ cups
vanilla extract	4 tsp	2 Tbsp	1 tsp	2 tsp
large eggs	6	10	3	4
large egg yolks	6	8	2	4
sour cream	1⅓ cups plus 1 Tbsp	2 cups	½ cup	¾ cup plus 2 Tbsp
baking powder	1 Tbsp	4 tsp	1 tsp	1 tsp
cocoa powder, sifted	1 cup	1⅓ cups	⅓ cup	⅔ cup
self-rising flour, sifted	3½ cups	5 cups	1⅓ cups	2¼ cups
For the chocolate buttercream				
dark chocolate chips	1 cup plus 2 Tbsp	1¾ cups	⅓ cup plus 1 Tbsp	½ cup plus 1 Tbsp
unsalted butter, softened	1¾ cups	2¼ cups	⅔ cup	¾ cup plus 2 Tbsp
confectioners' sugar, sifted	6⅓ cups	8 cups	2 cups plus 6 Tbsp	3¼ cups
sour cream	7 Tbsp	½ cup plus 2 Tbsp	3 Tbsp	¼ cup
Baking time @ 350°F	45 to 55 mins	50 mins to 1 hour	1 hour	45 to 55 mins

A classic roulade is made without flour, making it gluten-free. Add berries to the whipped cream filling, or ripple the cream with chocolate hazelnut spread or dulce de leche for a decadent dessert.

Chocolate Roulade

8 oz 70% dark chocolate, broken into small pieces
8 extra-large eggs, separated
1 cup plus 2 Tbsp granulated sugar
4 tsp cocoa powder
1½ cups heavy cream, whipped to soft peaks
confectioners' sugar, for dusting

YOU WILL NEED
9 x 13-inch baking pan, greased, then lined with parchment paper
14-inch-long sheet of parchment paper

1 Heat the oven to 350°F. Melt the chocolate in a bowl set over a pot of simmering water. Stir until smooth, then remove from the heat and cool slightly.

2 Whisk the egg yolks and granulated sugar in the bowl of a stand mixer fitted with the whisk attachment, on high speed, until the mixture is thick and mousse-like, and leaves a ribbon trail when you lift the whisk.

3 In a separate, clean, grease-free bowl, whisk the egg whites to stiff (but not dry) peaks, using an electric hand mixer.

4 Pour the chocolate mixture into the egg-yolk mixture and fold together with a large metal spoon. Add 1 large spoonful of egg whites and fold to loosen.

5 Carefully fold in the remaining egg whites, then sift the cocoa powder over the top and fold until completely combined.

6 Pour the mixture into the prepared pan and gently tip the pan so that the mixture flows into the corners and is level. Bake for 20 to 25 minutes, until risen and slightly crisp. Remove from the oven and place on a wire rack to cool in the pan.

7 Lay the sheet of parchment paper on the work surface and sprinkle with confectioners' sugar. Turn out the roulade onto the sugar-coated paper. Peel away the parchment paper that was lining the pan.

8 Turn the roulade so that one of the short ends is closest to you. Using a sharp knife, score a shallow cut ¾ inch in from the closest short end. Spread the roulade with the cream leaving a ¾-inch border around the edge. Using the paper to help, gently roll up the roulade. (It's normal for the roulade to crack.)

9 Roll until the seam is underneath, then transfer to a serving plate and dust with confectioners' sugar before serving.

This spectacular snake cake is sure to cause a sensation at any birthday party. The netting from a bag of store-bought citrus fruit provides the perfect template for the scaly skin.

Snakey Birthday Cakey

FOR THE SPONGE
1¼ cups boiling water
3½ oz 70% dark chocolate, very finely chopped
1 tsp baking soda
¾ cup plus 2 Tbsp unsalted butter, softened
1¾ cups granulated sugar
¾ cup plus 1 Tbsp condensed milk
20 drops of orange oil
finely grated zest of 1 unwaxed orange
2 Tbsp glycerin
4 extra-large eggs, beaten
3¼ cups cake flour
4 tsp baking powder
⅔ cup cocoa powder
½ tsp salt

FOR THE FONDANT ICING
6 Tbsp cold water
3 Tbsp gelatin powder
½ cup plus 1 Tbsp glucose syrup
¼ cup glycerin
10¾ cups confectioners' sugar, sifted
light green food-coloring gel
dark green food-coloring gel
red food-coloring gel
yellow food-coloring gel

FOR THE CHOCOLATE MERINGUE BUTTERCREAM
5¼ oz 70% dark chocolate
4 extra-large egg whites
1 cup plus 2 Tbsp granulated sugar
⅔ cup plus 1 Tbsp unsalted butter, diced, softened

1 Heat the oven to 350°F.

2 For the sponge, pour the boiling water into a pitcher, add the chocolate and stir to melt, then stir in the baking soda.

3 Beat the butter, sugar, condensed milk, orange oil, and orange zest in the bowl of a stand mixer fitted with the paddle attachment, on medium speed for 1 minute, until smooth. With the mixer still running, add the glycerin and eggs, and mix until well combined.

4 In a separate bowl, sift together the flour, baking powder, cocoa, and salt. With the mixer on medium speed, add half the flour mixture and mix until combined, then add the watery chocolate mixture, then the remaining flour mixture and combine for 1 to 2 minutes to a smooth batter.

5 Fill the two cupcake liners three-quarters full, then divide the remaining batter evenly between the two cake pans. Bake the cupcakes for 25 to 30 minutes and the cakes for 40 to 45 minutes, until a skewer inserted into the centers comes out clean. Let cool in the pans for 5 minutes, then transfer to a wire rack to cool completely.

6 For the fondant icing, pour the cold water into a small bowl, then sprinkle the gelatin over the water and let rest for 3 minutes, until bloomed.

7 In a small pot, simmer the glucose for 30 seconds, then add the gelatin and glycerin, stirring until dissolved. Tip the confectioners' sugar into a bowl and pour in the glucose mixture. Mix with a spatula, then bring everything together with your hands and knead it gently to a smooth fondant. Wrap the icing in plastic wrap and set aside.

ingredients and recipe continue

FOR THE CRISPED-RICE SCULPTURE
2 Tbsp unsalted butter
3½ oz white marshmallows
3 cups crisped rice cereal

TO DECORATE
1 package snake gummies
pink edible luster spray
gold edible luster spray

YOU WILL NEED
6- or 12-cup muffin tin, lined
     with 2 cupcake paper liners
9-inch springform cake pans x 2,
     greased, then base-lined with
     parchment paper
large piping bag fitted with
     a large plain nozzle
2-inch round cutter
wooden skewers
cake-decorating paintbrush
netting from a bag of citrus fruit

8 For the chocolate meringue buttercream, melt the chocolate in a bowl set over a pot of gently simmering water. Stir, then remove from the heat and let cool.

9 Place the egg whites and sugar in a bowl set over a pot of simmering water and stir to dissolve the sugar. Pour the mixture into the bowl of a stand mixer fitted with the whisk attachment and whisk to a thick, glossy meringue. Whisk in the cooled, melted chocolate, then add the butter, little by little, and whisk to a smooth, fluffy buttercream. Spoon half the mixture into the piping bag and set aside.

10 To assemble, carve the round cakes to become the main body of the snake, sitting one on top of the other. Using the 2-inch round cutter, cut out the center of the cake, leaving a hole in the middle. Sandwich the cakes together with some of the buttercream in the bowl, then cover the cake in a crumb coat and chill in the refrigerator for 20 minutes.

11 Hollow out the two cupcakes and fill them with snake gummies. Stick them together with some of the buttercream in the bowl, then carve them to make an egg shape. Cover in a thin layer of buttercream to create a crumb coat and chill for 20 minutes.

12 For the crisped-rice sculpture, place the butter and marshmallows in a pot over low heat, stirring until melted. Remove from the heat and stir in the crisped rice and mix until coated. Chill to a molding consistency (about 30 minutes).

13 Once moldable, wet your hands and use some of the crisped rice to shape a little tail that sticks up, and the remainder to create a head shape that fits on the top of the cake. Place the pieces on a plate and chill to firm up.

14 Remove the cake from the fridge and use a skewer to secure the tail to the bottom end of the snake shape, then pipe the buttercream all over the cake. Smooth over with an offset spatula and chill again for 20 minutes.

15 While the cake is chilling, color two-thirds of the fondant light green. On a surface lightly dusted with confectioners' sugar, roll out two-thirds of the green fondant to a large circle, big enough to cover the cake, reserving the remaining green fondant for the head.

16 Carefully cover the cake with the circle of green fondant, molding it between the two cakes to form the coils. Using a cake-decorating paintbrush with some watered-down green food coloring, paint along the creases of the snake coils to make a shadow.

17 Lay the citrus-bag netting over the cake and spray the fondant with pink and gold luster spray to create a scale effect.

18 Roll out half the remaining white fondant and use this to cover the cupcake "egg." Use the netting again as a template and spray with gold luster spray. Using the white fondant trimmings, shape the snake's teeth—mold them around the tips of a few skewers and pinch the ends to create the points.

19 Roll out the remaining green fondant and use this to cover the snake's head.

20 Color half the remaining white fondant dark green and the other half red, reserving a marble-sized piece of white fondant to color yellow.

21 Roll out the dark green fondant and cut out pieces for around the eyes and for the collar. Make two eyes out of a little bit of red and yellow fondant and stick them in place with water, then add the green pieces around the eyes.

22 Roll out the remaining red fondant and use this to line the inside of the mouth, reserving a little to make the tongue. Insert skewers halfway into the back of the head and attach the head to the main cake, then use water to stick on the fondant collar pieces to hide the seam.

23 Insert the teeth into the snake's head, then make a red tongue with the reserved red fondant and stick it in the mouth. Fill the inside coil of the cake with the remaining buttercream and place the "egg" on top.

Andrew's hazelnuts dipped in caramel (from Season 7) may seem like an effort, but they are worth it—not only do they look impressive, they give a crunch to each slice.

Andrew

Orange, Salted Caramel & Chocolate Mirror Glaze Cake

FOR THE GÉNOISE
5 large eggs
¾ cup plus 1 Tbsp granulated sugar
1⅔ cups all-purpose flour
finely grated zest of 2 large unwaxed oranges
a pinch of salt
3 Tbsp unsalted butter, melted, plus extra for greasing

FOR THE SALTED CARAMEL SAUCE
¼ cup unsalted butter
⅔ cup light muscovado sugar
2½ cups heavy cream
1 tsp flaky sea salt

FOR THE CHOCOLATE MIRROR GLAZE
½ cup plus 2 Tbsp heavy cream
⅔ cup granulated sugar
⅔ cup cocoa powder
3 gelatin sheets

TO DECORATE
¼ cup granulated sugar
8 blanched hazelnuts
chocolate curls (optional)

YOU WILL NEED
8-inch springform pans x 2, greased, then base-lined with parchment paper
8-inch cake card
toothpicks or wooden skewers

1 Heat the oven to 350°F.

2 For the génoise, whisk the eggs and sugar in the bowl of a stand mixer fitted with the whisk attachment, on high speed, until the mixture is thick and mousse-like and leaves a ribbon trail when you lift the whisk.

3 Sift the flour into the mixture one third at a time, gently folding in each batch before adding the next. Fold in the orange zest and salt. Slowly pour the melted butter down the side of the bowl and fold in with a large metal spoon.

4 Divide the mixture equally between the prepared cake pans, and bake for 18 to 20 minutes, or until a skewer inserted in the centers comes out clean. Cool in the pans for 5 minutes, then transfer to a wire rack to cool completely.

5 For the salted caramel sauce, place the butter and sugar in a small pot over low heat and stir for 3 to 4 minutes, until the sugar has melted. Drizzle in 5 tablespoons of the cream, mixing well. Bring to a simmer for 1 minute, then remove from the heat. Stir in the sea salt and set aside, stirring occasionally, until cool.

6 Using an electric hand mixer, whisk the remaining 2 cups plus 3 tablespoons of cream until it forms soft peaks, then gently whisk in the cooled salted caramel.

7 To assemble the cake, using a large serrated knife, cut each cake in half horizontally to make four layers. Carefully place the first layer on the cake card. Using an offset spatula, spread about a ¼-inch layer of cream on top. Top with a layer of sponge and repeat the cream and cake layers until you have four layers of génoise with salted caramel cream on top of each layer.

recipe continues

8 Using the spatula, apply a thin crumb coat of cream all over the cake, filling any gaps to create a smooth surface. Chill for 20 minutes.

9 Reserve about 5 tablespoons of the cream for decoration, then add a thick layer of cream all over the cake, smoothing neatly. Chill for 20 minutes, until the cream is firm.

10 For the chocolate mirror glaze, place the cream, sugar, cocoa powder, and ½ cup plus 2 tablespoons of water in a small pot and heat gently, stirring to dissolve the sugar. Bring to a simmer for 2 minutes, then remove from the heat and let cool for 10 minutes.

11 Soak the gelatin sheets in cold water for 5 minutes. Squeeze any excess water from the sheets and stir them into the glaze until dissolved. Pass the glaze through a fine sieve into a measuring cup and tap on a hard surface to remove any air bubbles. Let cool until thick, like pourable custard.

12 Transfer the cake to a wire rack set over a large baking sheet. Pour the glaze evenly over the top and down the sides of the cake. Chill the cake for 1 hour to set the glaze.

13 To decorate, put the sugar and 2 tablespoons of water in a small pan over medium heat. Swirl the pan to help the sugar caramelize but do not stir. Heat for 3 to 4 minutes, until the sugar is an amber color, then remove from the heat.

14 Attach each hazelnut to the end of a toothpick or wooden skewer. Very carefully dip each hazelnut into the caramel and hang it over the edge of a work surface, using a heavy chopping board to hold the sticks in place (protect the floor with newspaper). Once you've coated all the hazelnuts, use scissors to trim the caramel spikes to the same length and remove the nuts from the sticks onto a sheet of parchment paper.

15 Place the cake on a serving plate and pipe 8 small circles of salted caramel cream around the edge. Put a caramelized hazelnut on each circle. Pile chocolate curls in the center, if using.

These small but perfectly formed cakes are traditionally made with ground almonds, but in this recipe the hazelnuts, once combined with the browned butter, add an irresistible depth. This recipe is quick to make—you can have a tempting batch of financiers ready within 30 minutes.

Hazelnut & Chocolate Financiers

⅓ cup unsalted butter, diced
⅓ cup granulated sugar
½ cup ground hazelnuts
⅓ cup cocoa powder
3 Tbsp all-purpose flour, sifted
1 Tbsp honey
2 extra-large egg whites

TO DECORATE
3 Tbsp chocolate hazelnut
  spread, melted
2 Tbsp chopped hazelnuts

YOU WILL NEED
medium disposable
  piping bag (optional)
16-cup silicone mold
  (shape of your choice),
  or a greased, nonstick
  12-cup muffin tin

1 Heat the oven to 425°F.

2 Melt the diced butter in a small pot over medium-high heat for 5 to 10 minutes, until it starts to turn brown at the bottom and smells like popcorn. Remove from the heat and set aside.

3 In a bowl whisk together the sugar, ground hazelnuts, cocoa powder, and flour. Add the honey and egg whites and whisk until well combined.

4 Pour the melted brown butter into the bowl with the sugar mixture and whisk again until completely combined.

5 Spoon the mixture into the piping bag, if using, and snip a ½-inch hole in the end. Pipe equal amounts of the mixture into the cups of your silicone mold or greased muffin tin. Alternatively, simply spoon in the mixture in equal amounts.

6 Bake the financiers for 10 to 15 minutes, until a skewer inserted into the centers comes out clean. Remove the pan from the oven and place it on a wire rack to allow the cakes to cool.

7 Use a small spoon to drizzle each financier with a little melted hazelnut spread and sprinkle a few chopped hazelnuts on top.

HOW TO...
DECORATE WITH CHOCOLATE

The first and most important rule for decorating with chocolate is that whatever chocolate you're using— white, milk, or dark—always use the best quality available.

MELTING CHOCOLATE

Melt your chocolate slowly over low heat. Overheated chocolate can scorch and separate or, in the case of milk or white chocolate, turn grainy or lumpy—this is technically known as seizing (white chocolate is particularly sensitive to heat). There are two ways to melt chocolate: in a bowl over a pot of water or in a microwave.

METHOD 1 Break the chocolate into small, even-sized pieces and place the pieces in a heatproof bowl. Set the bowl over a pot that is one-third full with gently simmering or steaming water, making sure that the bottom of the bowl doesn't touch the water. Turn the heat to low, or turn it off completely, and just let the chocolate melt, occasionally giving it a stir to help it, if you like. When it's melted carefully lift the bowl off the pan.

METHOD 2 Break the chocolate into pieces as for method 1. Microwave dark chocolate on 50 percent power in 30-second bursts, until melted. Stir the chocolate after each burst. Microwave milk and white chocolate in the same way but at 30 percent power.

TEMPERING CHOCOLATE

Tempering your chocolate is a process of heating and cooling chocolate to a particular temperature (you'll need a candy thermometer) to produce chocolate that is shiny and has a good snap. It is perfect for coating cakes, or making chocolate decorations and filled chocolates.

There are two basic ways to temper chocolate:

METHOD 1 Follow the process for melting chocolate, opposite. Melt two thirds of the chocolate until a candy thermometer reaches 113°F for dark chocolate or 109°F for milk or white. Remove from the heat, then stir in the remaining third of the chocolate until melted. Let cool, continuing to stir, until the temperature reaches 80°F.

METHOD 2 Follow the process for melting chocolate, opposite. Melt all the chocolate until a candy thermometer reaches 113°F for dark chocolate or 109°F for milk or white. Remove from the heat and pour two-thirds of the melted chocolate onto a dry marble slab or work surface. With an offset spatula, work the chocolate by spreading it back and forth until it thickens and becomes difficult to spread. Scrape this into the remaining melted chocolate and stir. Gently reheat the chocolate until it reaches 88°F for dark chocolate or 80°F for milk or white.

MAKING CHOCOLATE GANACHE

Ganache is a combination of dark chocolate and cream and is perfect for filling or frosting cakes—or for making rich chocolate truffles. A ganache will keep in the fridge for up to 1 week.

The rule of thumb for a soft ganache frosting is to use one part dark chocolate to two parts cream. For a cake filling, use equal weights of chocolate and cream.

1 Break the chocolate into small, even-sized pieces and place in a heatproof bowl.

2 Heat the cream in a pot over medium-low heat to just below the boiling point, then pour it into the bowl over the chocolate.

3 Stir until the chocolate melts, then set aside to cool and thicken before use. Alternatively, once the ganache is cool, whisk it with an electric hand mixer until light, creamy, and mousse-like.

Making chocolate decorations

For the best results, use tempered chocolate (see page 93) for making chocolate decorations, although simple melted chocolate can work, too.

CURLS

Pour the tempered or melted chocolate onto a marble slab, work surface, or baking sheet. Spread the chocolate as smoothly as possible into a thin, even layer using a flexible spatula or offset spatula. Let the chocolate cool at room temperature, until nearly set. Then, as soon as the chocolate is firm but still pliable, scrape the edge of an offset spatula away from you at a 45-degree angle to roll the chocolate into cylinders or curls.

LEAVES

Using a small brush, paint the underside of washed and dried rose leaves (leave a little bit of stem to help with the peeling later), or other edible leaves, with a layer (or several layers) of tempered chocolate. Place the coated leaves on parchment paper and let cool and set, then, starting at the stem end, carefully peel away the leaf from the chocolate. Attach the chocolate leaves to cakes or chocolate flowers with a little melted chocolate, royal icing, or edible glue.

PIPED DECORATIONS

Tempered chocolate can be piped onto parchment paper, nonstick acetate, or a silicone mat into the decorative shape of your choice, including words, trees, flowers, hearts, spirals, or swirls.

Fill a small disposable piping bag with tempered chocolate and snip off the tip, then pipe your design on a sheet of parchment paper or acetate. (Either pipe the chocolate freehand or draw a template on a piece of paper, then place it under the parchment paper or acetate to follow as you pipe.)

Let the chocolate set firmly at room temperature or in the fridge. Then peel the designs off the paper or acetate with an offset spatula and use immediately, or store, layered between sheets of parchment paper, in an airtight container in a cool place.

Begin the salted caramel for these heavenly brownies at least 2 hours before you intend to bake, so that it has time to cool and firm up.

Chocolate & Salted Caramel Brownies

FOR THE SALTED CARAMEL
¾ cup plus 1 Tbsp granulated
   sugar
½ cup plus 1 Tbsp heavy cream
2 tsp flaky sea salt,
   plus extra for sprinkling
3 Tbsp unsalted butter, diced

FOR THE BROWNIE
12 oz 70% dark chocolate,
   broken into pieces
¾ cup unsalted butter
4 large eggs
1¾ cups light muscovado sugar
½ cup granulated sugar
1 tsp vanilla extract
1⅔ cups all-purpose flour
3 Tbsp cocoa powder
a pinch of salt

YOU WILL NEED
9-inch square cake pan,
   greased, then lined (base and
   sides) with parchment paper

1 For the salted caramel, melt the sugar in a medium pot over medium heat. Swirl the pan without stirring for 8 to 10 minutes, until the caramel has turned a dark amber color.

2 In a separate pot, bring the cream to a boil, then immediately remove it from the heat and set aside.

3 Remove the caramel from the heat and carefully add the salt and half the cream. (Take care as the mixture will spit.) Once the mixture has settled, add the remaining cream and the butter, and stir together. Return the pan to the heat and cook for 2 minutes, stirring, until thick and smooth.

4 Pour the salted caramel into a bowl. Let cool, then cover with plastic wrap and chill for at least 2 hours, until firm but spoonable. When the caramel is almost ready, start the brownies. Heat the oven to 350°F.

5 Melt the chocolate and butter together in a bowl set over a pot of simmering water, stirring occasionally for 4 to 5 minutes, until smooth. Remove from the heat and set aside to cool.

6 Using an electric hand mixer, in a large bowl whisk together the eggs and both sugars until thick and pale. Whisk the cooled chocolate mixture and the vanilla into the egg mixture, then sift in the flour, cocoa powder, and salt. Fold together until well mixed.

7 Pour the mixture into the prepared pan and level with the back of a spoon. Spoon the caramel onto the brownie mixture and sprinkle with a little sea salt.

8 Bake for 45 to 50 minutes, or until a skewer inserted into the center comes out sticky (but not wet). Allow to cool in the pan completely, then remove from the pan and use a hot knife to cut it into squares.

Start the brown butter at least an hour before you intend to bake this cake. If you have four cake pans, you can halve the baking time by making the four sponges in one stage rather than two.

Chocolate Drip Cake

FOR THE BROWN BUTTER SPONGE
1 cup plus 2 Tbsp unsalted butter, diced
1 cup plus 1 Tbsp light muscovado sugar
4 large eggs
1¾ cups self-rising flour, sifted
1 tsp baking powder

FOR THE CHOCOLATE SPONGE
¾ cup plus 2 Tbsp unsalted butter, softened
1 cup granulated sugar
1 tsp vanilla extract
4 large eggs
⅔ cup cocoa powder
2 Tbsp whole milk
1⅔ cups self-rising flour, sifted

FOR THE BUTTERCREAM
7 oz 70% dark chocolate
7 Tbsp heavy cream
2¼ cups unsalted butter, softened
2 tsp vanilla extract
8 cups confectioners' sugar, sifted

FOR THE SHARDS
3½ oz 70% dark chocolate
3½ oz white chocolate
edible gold leaf (optional)

TO DECORATE
7 oz 70% dark chocolate, melted
strawberries, raspberries, or cherries (or a mixture)
edible gold spray (optional)

1 Make the brown butter sponges: Melt the butter in a pot over medium-high heat, reduce the heat, and simmer for 8 to 10 minutes, until the butter starts to brown and smell like popcorn. Let cool, then chill for 1 to 2 hours, until set.

2 Heat the oven to 400°F. Beat the cooled brown butter and the sugar in the bowl of a stand mixer fitted with the paddle attachment, on medium speed for 2 to 3 minutes, until creamy.

3 With the mixer on low speed, add the eggs, one at a time, beating well after each addition. Add the flour and baking powder, mixing until combined. Divide the mixture equally between the pans and bake for 20 to 25 minutes, until a skewer inserted into the centers comes out clean. Let cool in the pans for 5 minutes, then turn out onto a wire rack to cool completely.

4 Make the chocolate sponges: Re-line the pans. Beat the butter, sugar, and vanilla together in the bowl of a stand mixer fitted with the paddle attachment, on medium speed for 2 to 3 minutes, until pale and creamy. With the mixer on low speed, add the eggs, one at a time, beating well after each addition.

5 Combine the cocoa powder and milk in a small bowl, then add to the batter and beat on medium speed for 30 to 60 seconds, until combined. With the mixer on low speed, add the flour, and beat until just combined. Divide the mixture equally between the pans and bake for 20 to 25 minutes, until a skewer inserted into the centers comes out clean. Let cool in the pans for 5 minutes, then turn out onto a wire rack to cool completely.

6 Make the buttercream: Put the chocolate and cream in a bowl set over a pot of simmering water. Stir for 2 to 3 minutes to a smooth ganache. Remove from the heat and let cool.

7 Beat the butter and vanilla in the bowl of a stand mixer fitted with the paddle attachment, on high speed for about 1 minute,

ingredients and recipe continue

YOU WILL NEED
8-inch round cake pans x 2, greased, then lined (base and sides) with parchment paper
large baking sheet, lined with parchment paper
medium disposable piping bag

until very creamy and smooth. Add the confectioners' sugar, one quarter at a time, beating slowly at first, then increasing the speed for 1 minute. Slowly add the cooled ganache and beat until fluffy. Spoon one third of the buttercream into a separate bowl and set aside.

8 To assemble, level the sponges. Put a dab of buttercream on a cake plate, then top with a brown-butter sponge. Cover with one fifth of the larger portion of buttercream. Top with a chocolate sponge and spread with a fifth of the buttercream. Repeat for the second brown-butter sponge and another fifth of the buttercream. Place the final chocolate sponge on top.

9 Spread another one fifth of the buttercream around the side of the cake, and the final fifth evenly over the top. Smooth off any excess to create a crumb coat. Chill for 1 hour.

10 Repeat the buttercream process using two thirds of the reserved buttercream to create a thick, even coating. (Set aside the remaining buttercream for attaching the decorations.) Chill the cake while you make the chocolate shards.

11 Melt the dark and white chocolates in separate bowls set over pots of simmering water. Pour the dark chocolate randomly on the lined baking sheet, then pour on the white, filling any gaps. Drag a toothpick through to marble.

12 Bang the sheet firmly on the work surface to get rid of any air bubbles, then let set. Add gold leaf to the chocolate as it sets, if you wish. Once set, use a knife to cut it into shards.

13 Make the decoration: Melt the dark chocolate in a bowl set over a pot of simmering water. Remove from the heat and let cool for 2 to 3 minutes.

14 Pour the chocolate into the piping bag and cut a small, ¼-inch hole in the end. To pipe the drip, hold the bag at the top of the cake and steadily move around the edge, allowing the drips to trail down the sides, varying your squeeze to achieve different lengths. Pipe chocolate over the top of the cake, and spread it evenly with an offset spatula.

15 Use the remaining buttercream to attach the shards, fruit, and gold-sprayed cherries, as well as extra pieces of gold leaf, if you wish.

Take your time with this cake, and remember that buttercream is forgiving (you can scrape it off and start again!). Keep the cut-out parts of the cake to eat with ice cream, or make them into cake pops.

Chocolate Piñata Cake

FOR THE SPONGE
2⅔ cups dark chocolate chips
2¾ cups unsalted butter, softened
4⅓ cups light muscovado sugar
1 Tbsp vanilla extract
12 large eggs, beaten
3⅓ cups all-purpose flour, sifted
about 3 handfuls mixed gummies and candies of choice, to fill

FOR THE BUTTERCREAM
4 cups unsalted butter, softened
1½ Tbsp vanilla extract
14¾ cups confectioners' sugar, sifted
light blue food-coloring paste
red food-coloring paste

YOU WILL NEED
9-inch round, deep cake pans x 3, greased, then lined (base and sides) with parchment paper
5-inch-diameter circular card template
9-inch cake card
3 large piping bags, each fitted with a small petal nozzle
cake turntable

1 Heat the oven to 350°F.

2 Melt the chocolate chips in a bowl set over a pot of simmering water. Remove from the heat, then let cool.

3 Meanwhile, beat the butter, sugar, and vanilla in the bowl of a stand mixer fitted with the paddle attachment, on medium speed for 2 to 3 minutes, until pale and creamy.

4 On low speed, add the eggs, a little at a time, beating well after each addition. Pour in the cooled, melted chocolate and mix together. Add the flour and mix until just combined.

5 Divide the mixture among the prepared pans and bake for 45 to 55 minutes, until a skewer inserted into the centers comes out a little sticky (but not wet). Cool completely in the pans.

6 Make the buttercream: Beat the butter and vanilla in the bowl of a stand mixer fitted with the paddle attachment, on medium speed for 1 minute, until fluffy. With the mixer on low speed, add the confectioners' sugar, one third at a time, then increase the speed to medium and beat for 2 minutes, until fluffy. Spoon one quarter of the buttercream into a separate bowl and set aside.

7 To assemble, level the sponges and stack two on top of each other. Place the card template on top of the stack and cut around it to create a hole through the centers of the two cakes to give you two cake rings.

8 Place one of the cake rings on the cake card. Using an offset spatula, spread half the reserved buttercream over the sponge ring. Top with the second ring, and spread with the remaining half of the reserved buttercream.

recipe continues

Chocolate **103**

9 Completely fill the cavity with gummies and candies, then place the final sponge on top, leveled-side down, to enclose. Use some of the remaining buttercream to create a smooth crumb coat, then chill the cake for 30 minutes.

10 Divide the remaining buttercream equally among three bowls. Color one portion light blue, another portion bright red, and leave the final portion white. Place each buttercream into a piping bag fitted with a petal nozzle.

11 Place the cake on a turntable. For the piñata ruffle, using the blue buttercream, hold the petal nozzle against the bottom of the cake, with the wider, fat point touching the cake and the thin part facing outward. Using a wiggly, wavy motion, pipe around the cake base. Repeat, moving up the cake, with ruffles of white and red buttercream. Keep going, one color at a time, all the way to the top of the cake.

12 Once you reach the top of the cake, continue piping ruffles in ever-decreasing concentric circles, until you get to the middle of the cake.

With three layers and topped with chocolate triangles, this gooey cake is simple to make—but also delicious and impressive. Scale down the quantities by one third for a two-layered version (keep the baking time the same).

Devil's Food Cake

FOR THE CHOCOLATE FUDGE FROSTING
¾ cup plus 2 Tbsp heavy cream
1½ cups plus 1 Tbsp unsalted butter
1 lb 54% dark chocolate, finely chopped

FOR THE SPONGE
¾ cup plus 3 Tbsp cocoa powder, sifted
¾ cup light brown sugar
2 tsp vanilla extract
1½ cups boiling water
¾ cup plus 2 Tbsp unsalted butter
1 cup plus 2 Tbsp granulated sugar
3 extra-large eggs, beaten
2⅔ cups all-purpose flour, sifted
1 tsp baking powder
1 tsp baking soda

TO DECORATE
5¼ oz 70% dark chocolate
edible gold spray

YOU WILL NEED
8-inch round cake pans x 3, greased, then base-lined with parchment paper
sheet of acetate

1 Make the chocolate fudge frosting: Pour the cream into a medium pot, add the butter, and heat, stirring occasionally, until the butter has melted. Bring the mixture to just below boiling, then remove it from the heat. Add the chocolate and whisk until smooth and glossy. Pour the frosting into a bowl and let set at room temperature, whisking occasionally.

2 Heat the oven to 350°F. Make the sponge. Whisk the cocoa, brown sugar, vanilla, and boiling water together in a bowl to dissolve the sugar. Set aside.

3 Beat the butter and granulated sugar in the bowl of a stand mixer fitted with the paddle attachment, on medium speed for 3 to 5 minutes, until pale and creamy. Add the eggs, a little at a time, mixing well after each addition. Beat in the flour, one third at a time, and add the baking powder and baking soda.

4 Fold in the chocolate mixture, then divide equally among the three pans. Bake for 25 to 30 minutes, until a skewer inserted into the centers comes out clean. Let cool in the pans for 5 minutes, then turn out onto wire racks to cool completely.

5 To decorate, melt the chocolate in a bowl set over a pot of simmering water. Remove from the heat. Lay the acetate on a cold work surface and pour the melted chocolate over. Spread the chocolate until it starts to change color and begins to set. Use a knife to score triangular shapes. Transfer the acetate to a baking sheet. Freeze until the chocolate has set hard.

6 Place one sponge on a cake plate and spread with about one quarter of the frosting. Top with another sponge and spread as before. Place the remaining sponge on top, then spread and swirl the top and sides with the remaining frosting.

7 Peel away the acetate and arrange the chocolate triangles on top of the cake. Spray with edible gold spray.

These cousins of the brownies are quick and easy to make—which is good, as they are incredibly delicious and one batch is unlikely to last very long!

White Chocolate & Hazelnut Blondies

1 cup plus 2 Tbsp all-purpose flour, sifted
1 cup ground hazelnuts
a pinch of flaky sea salt
1 tsp baking powder
¾ cup plus 1 Tbsp unsalted butter, diced
¾ cup plus 2 Tbsp granulated sugar
1 cup light muscovado sugar
3 large eggs, beaten
2 tsp vanilla extract
¾ cup plus 3 Tbsp hazelnuts, chopped
¾ cup plus 3 Tbsp white chocolate chips
2 Tbsp honey or agave syrup

YOU WILL NEED
8½-inch square baking pan, greased, then lined (base and sides) with parchment paper

1 Heat the oven to 400°F.

2 Put the flour, ground hazelnuts, sea salt, and baking powder in a large bowl.

3 Melt the butter in a large bowl set over a pot of simmering water. Remove from the heat and stir in the granulated sugar and muscovado sugar.

4 Add the eggs, a little at a time, and the vanilla extract, then fold in the flour mixture until fully combined.

5 Gently fold in ½ cup plus 1 tablespoon of the chopped nuts and all the chocolate chips until evenly distributed, then pour the mixture into the prepared baking pan, giving the pan a gentle shake to disperse the mixture evenly.

6 Bake for 25 to 30 minutes, until a skewer inserted into the center comes out sticky (but not wet). Remove from the oven, brush with the honey or agave syrup, and sprinkle with the reserved chopped hazelnuts while the blondie is still warm.

7 Let the blondie cool in the pan for 10 minutes, then remove it carefully and transfer it to a wire rack to cool completely before slicing into squares.

Flora's stunning reinvention of the Black Forest gâteau in Season 6—left naked on the side to partly reveal the tempting filling—has a magical forest of truffles, chocolate trees, and cherry jellies.

Flora

Black Forest Gâteau

FOR THE CHOCOLATE SPONGE
3½ oz 70% dark chocolate, chopped
¾ cup boiling water
¼ cup cocoa powder
½ cup plus 1 Tbsp unsalted butter, softened
1¾ cups granulated sugar
2 extra-large eggs, beaten
1 tsp baking soda
1 tsp vanilla extract
2⅓ cups all-purpose flour, sifted
½ cup heavy cream

FOR THE CHERRY SPONGE
1 cup unsalted butter, softened
1 cup plus 2 Tbsp granulated sugar
red food-coloring paste
2 tsp freeze-dried sour cherry powder
4 extra-large eggs, beaten
2 cups self-rising flour, sifted
2 to 4 Tbsp whole milk

FOR THE CHOCOLATE TRUFFLES
3½ oz 70% dark chocolate, chopped
1 Tbsp kirsch
7 Tbsp heavy cream
½ tsp vanilla extract
2 Tbsp unsweetened shredded coconut
1 Tbsp freeze-dried sour cherry powder

1 For the chocolate sponge, heat the oven to 350°F. Mix together the chocolate, boiling water, and cocoa in a bowl until melted and smooth. Set aside.

2 Beat the butter and sugar in the bowl of a stand mixer fitted with the paddle attachment, on medium speed for 5 minutes, until pale and creamy. On low speed, gradually beat in the eggs, then the baking soda, vanilla, flour, cream, and finally the chocolate mixture. Divide the mixture between the pans and bake for 35 to 40 minutes, until risen and firm to the touch. Cool in the pans for 10 minutes, then turn out onto a wire rack to cool completely. Wash, grease, and re-line the pans.

3 For the cherry sponge, beat the butter and sugar in the bowl of a stand mixer fitted with the paddle attachment, on medium speed for 5 minutes, until pale and creamy. Add enough food coloring and the cherry powder to give it a deep red color, then slowly beat in the eggs with a little flour. Fold in the remaining flour and the milk. Divide the mixture between the pans and bake for 25 to 30 minutes, until risen and firm. Cool in the pans for 10 minutes, then turn out onto a wire rack to cool completely.

4 For the truffles, place the chocolate in a heatproof bowl with the kirsch. Bring the cream and vanilla to a boil in a heavy-bottomed pot, then pour half the mixture on top of the chocolate and stir. Stir in the remaining cream mixture.

5 Pour the chocolate mixture into a shallow dish and chill to set. Then use a spoon to scoop out balls and roll some in the coconut and some in the cherry powder. Store in the fridge.

6 For the cherry jellies, place the cherries, lemon juice, and sugar in a small pot with 3 tablespoons of water. Bring to a boil, remove from the heat, and blitz using an immersion blender until finely chopped. Then pour the mixture through a sieve into a clean pot and stir in the agar-agar.

ingredients and recipe continue

FOR THE CHERRY JELLIES
½ cup cherries, pitted
3 Tbsp lemon juice
3 Tbsp granulated sugar
¼ tsp agar-agar

FOR THE CHOCOLATE TREES
3½ oz 70% dark chocolate,
    chopped
1 tsp freeze-dried cherry
    pieces, plus extra to decorate

FOR THE CHOCOLATE SAUCE
1¾ oz 70% dark chocolate,
    chopped
2 Tbsp unsalted butter
½ cup heavy cream
1 Tbsp granulated sugar

FOR THE BUTTERCREAM
4½ oz white chocolate,
    chopped
¾ cup plus 1 Tbsp unsalted
    butter, softened
3¼ cups confectioners' sugar,
    sifted
1 tsp vanilla extract
3 Tbsp whole milk

TO DECORATE
1¼ cups heavy cream
1 tsp vanilla extract
3 Tbsp kirsch
1¾ cups cherries, half pitted
    and quartered; half left whole
confectioners' sugar, for
    dusting

YOU WILL NEED
8-inch round, deep cake pans
    x 2, greased, then base-lined
    with parchment paper
1¼-inch round cutter
small disposable piping bag
baking sheet lined with
    parchment paper
large disposable piping bag

7 Place the pot over high heat and boil until the agar-agar dissolves completely. Pour into a shallow container to about ¾ inch deep and chill for 1 hour to set. Use the 1¼-inch cutter to create the jelly disks for decoration.

8 For the chocolate trees, melt the chocolate in a small bowl set over a pot of simmering water. Beat until smooth, then pour the chocolate into the small piping bag. Snip the end and pipe tree shapes of various sizes onto the lined baking sheet. Sprinkle with dried cherry pieces and chill for at least 15 minutes to set.

9 For the chocolate sauce, melt all the ingredients together in a small pot over low heat, stir until smooth, then set aside.

10 For the buttercream, melt the white chocolate in a small bowl set over a pot of simmering water. Let cool slightly.

11 Beat the butter in the bowl of a stand mixer fitted with the paddle attachment, on high speed until very pale. Add the confectioners' sugar and beat for 5 minutes, until almost white. Add the melted chocolate, vanilla, and milk and beat until smooth. Spoon into the large piping bag and snip a ¾-inch hole in the end.

12 In a bowl, whip the cream and vanilla for the decoration with an electric hand mixer to soft peaks.

13 To assemble, brush all the cake layers with some kirsch. Pipe a little buttercream on a cake plate and top with a chocolate sponge. Pipe large dots of buttercream all the way around the edge of this and the other chocolate layer and on one of the cherry layers. Spread chocolate sauce in the middle of each buttercream ring. Top with quartered cherries, then spread with a little cream until level with the buttercream dots.

14 For the second cherry sponge, pipe a dot of buttercream then drag the piping bag into the center of the cake to create a droplet shape. Repeat all the way around the cake.

15 Place the first cherry sponge on top of the chocolate sponge on the stand. Add the second chocolate sponge and finish with the cherry layer with the buttercream design. Add the trees on top of the cake, along with some truffles, fresh whole cherries, and the little disks of jelly. Dust with confectioners' sugar and extra dried cherry pieces. Serve with the remaining truffles.

Once you've tried these, you'll never go back to store-bought versions. They need a little skill in the rolling but are otherwise really easy to make.

Chocolate Mini Rolls

FOR THE SPONGE
¾ cup plus 3 Tbsp cocoa powder, sifted
3 Tbsp unsalted butter, melted
1¼ tsp vanilla extract
5 Tbsp boiling water
1 cup granulated sugar
8 extra-large eggs, separated

FOR THE FILLING
¾ cup plus 1 Tbsp unsalted butter, softened
3 cups confectioners' sugar, sifted
1¼ tsp peppermint extract

TO DECORATE
9 oz 70% dark chocolate
9 oz milk chocolate
4½ oz white chocolate

YOU WILL NEED
9 x 13-inch baking pans x 2, greased, then base-lined with greased parchment paper
2 sheets of parchment paper
small disposable piping bag

1 Heat the oven to 350°F. Make the sponge: Combine the cocoa powder, butter, vanilla, and boiling water in a small bowl. Set aside.

2 Whisk together ½ cup of the granulated sugar and the egg yolks in a separate bowl, until pale, thick, and fluffy. Add the chocolate mixture and whisk to combine.

3 In a separate bowl, using an electric hand mixer, whisk the egg whites to stiff peaks. Add the remaining sugar and whisk to dissolve. Beat one third of the meringue mixture into the chocolate mixture to loosen. Using a large metal spoon, fold in the remaining meringue mixture until fully combined.

4 Divide the mixture equally between the two prepared pans and level it out. Bake for 12 to 18 minutes, until springy to the touch. Place the pans on a wire rack, cover the sponges with a damp tea towel, and let cool completely.

5 Make the filling: With a wooden spoon, beat the butter in a bowl until soft, and gradually add the confectioners' sugar. Add the peppermint extract and beat until white, soft, and fluffy.

6 Invert each sponge onto a sheet of parchment paper. Peel off the top layer of parchment paper. Turn the sponges so the short ends are facing you. Score a line 1½ inches in from the nearest short end of each sponge. Spread the filling evenly over each sponge.

7 Take one sponge and, starting from the short edge closest to you, roll it up, stopping in the middle. Repeat from the edge farthest away, until both rolls meet in the middle. Cut down the center between the rolls.

recipe continues

8 Roll and cut the other sponge, so that you have four rolls. Trim the ends and cut each roll into thirds to create 12 mini rolls. Place the rolls, seam-sides down, on a wire rack and chill them for 15 minutes to firm up.

9 To finish, melt the dark and milk chocolates together in a bowl set over a pot of simmering water. Stir to combine.

10 Place the wire rack with the mini rolls over a baking sheet. Spread or pour the chocolate mixture over each mini roll to coat. Let set.

11 Melt the white chocolate in a bowl set over a pot of simmering water. Spoon the melted chocolate into the small disposable piping bag and snip a tiny hole in the end. Pipe fine stripes across the mini rolls, then let set.

John's epic showstopping creation from Season 3 is altogether divine—with lemon and coconut cakes representing heaven and the deeply indulgent chocolate cake representing hell.

John

Heaven & Hell Cake

FOR THE HELL CAKE
¾ cup cocoa powder
1 cup hot water
9 extra-large eggs, separated
½ cup plus 2 Tbsp sunflower oil
2½ tsp vanilla extract
2¼ cups granulated sugar
1½ tsp baking soda
1½ tsp salt
finely grated zest of 2 large
    unwaxed oranges
2½ cups plus 1 Tbsp
    all-purpose flour, sifted

FOR THE HEAVEN CAKES
3 extra-large eggs, separated
¼ cup sunflower oil
6 Tbsp chilled water
1 tsp vanilla extract
½ cup plus 2 Tbsp granulated
    sugar
finely grated zest of 1 large
    unwaxed lemon
1⅔ cups all-purpose flour,
    sifted
½ tsp baking powder
a pinch of salt
½ cup homemade or
    good-quality lemon curd

**FOR THE HELL GANACHE
& FILLING**
1¼ cups heavy cream
14 oz 54% dark chocolate,
    finely chopped
6 Tbsp homemade or
    good-quality cherry jam

1 Heat the oven to 325°F. For the hell cake, combine the cocoa powder and hot water until smooth. Set aside to cool a little. Place the egg yolks in a large bowl and, using a wooden spoon, stir in the oil, vanilla, sugar, baking soda, salt, and orange zest. Stir in the cooled cocoa mixture, then add the flour, beating until smooth.

2 Whisk the egg whites in the clean, grease-free bowl of a stand mixer fitted with the whisk, to stiff peaks. Fold the egg whites into the mixture, then spoon into the 10-inch pan. Level the top and bake for 1 hour 30 minutes, until a skewer inserted into the center comes out clean. Cool in the pan for 15 minutes, then turn out onto a wire rack to cool completely.

3 For the heaven cakes, place the egg yolks in a large bowl and, using a balloon whisk, mix in the oil, water, vanilla, sugar, lemon zest, flour, baking powder, and salt.

4 Whisk the egg whites in the clean, grease-free bowl of a stand mixer fitted with the whisk, to stiff peaks. Fold the egg whites into the mixture, then divide it equally among the mini pans. Bake for 15 to 17 minutes, until pale golden brown and just firm. Let cool in the pans for 15 minutes, then turn out onto a wire rack to cool completely. Then level the tops.

5 Spoon the lemon curd into the piping bag fitted with the jam nozzle and inject each small cake with lemon curd.

6 For the hell ganache, pour the cream into a medium pot over medium heat and bring just to a boil. Remove from the heat, add the chocolate and let stand for 5 minutes, then stir until smooth. Let cool until thick but spreadable.

7 Cut the chocolate cake in half horizontally. Spread the bottom half with the cherry jam and a little of the ganache, then top with the other cake half. Turn the whole cake upside down onto the large cake card.

ingredients and recipe continue

Heaven & Hell Cake *continued*

FOR THE HELL MIRROR GLAZE
¼ cup cold water
2 platinum-grade
   gelatin sheets
1 cup granulated sugar
2 Tbsp golden syrup or
   light corn syrup
1¾ cups cocoa powder, sifted
½ cup heavy cream

FOR THE HEAVEN MERINGUE & FILLING
2 extra-large egg whites
½ cup granulated sugar
¼ tsp cream of tartar
¼ tsp vanilla extract
1 cup plus 1 Tbsp unsweetened
   shredded coconut
5 sheets of edible gold leaf

TO DECORATE THE HELL CAKE
7 oz 54% dark chocolate

YOU WILL NEED
10-inch round, deep cake pan,
   greased, then base-lined
   with parchment paper
2-inch round mini-cake pans
   x 12, greased
medium piping bag fitted
   with a jam nozzle
12-inch cake card
2 medium piping bags,
   each fitted with a medium
   star nozzle
candy thermometer
6 straws or dowels
6-inch cake card
kitchen blowtorch
small piping bag fitted with
   a small writing nozzle
sheet of parchment paper
2 strips of parchment paper,
   each measuring 14 x 3 inches

8 Spread the top and sides with a thin layer of ganache, then chill for at least 10 minutes, or until set. Repeat with a second, thicker coat of ganache as neatly as possible. Chill again for another 15 minutes, until set. Spoon the remaining ganache into a medium piping bag fitted with a medium star nozzle and chill until thick enough to pipe.

9 For the hell mirror glaze, place the cold water in a shallow bowl, add the gelatin, and soak for 5 minutes. Boil the sugar in 7 tablespoons of water in a medium pot over high heat for about 3 minutes, stirring to dissolve. Let cool for 1 minute, then using a balloon whisk, stir in the golden syrup and cocoa until smooth. Squeeze out the gelatin and add it to the glaze, followed by the cream. Whisk until smooth. Place the chilled cake on a wire rack set over a baking sheet to catch the drips, and pour the glaze over the cake. Spread gently over the sides to cover.

10 For the heaven meringue, place the egg whites, sugar, and cream of tartar in a bowl set over a pot of simmering water. Whisk for 3 to 4 minutes, until it reaches 118°F on a candy thermometer. Remove from the pot and whisk until the mixture cools and forms stiff, shiny peaks. Whisk in the vanilla.

11 Cover the top and sides of each mini cake with meringue and roll in the coconut. Stack the cakes on the small cake card in a circle, seven cakes on the base, then four and then one on top, using straws or dowels to hold them in place. Place the remaining meringue in the remaining medium piping bag fitted with a medium star nozzle.

12 Place the small card on top of the chocolate cake and pipe swirls of meringue around the base of the card to cover it. Brown the piped meringue with a blowtorch until just golden. Decorate the heaven cakes with flakes of gold leaf.

13 To decorate the hell cake, temper the chocolate (see page 93), place a little into the small piping bag with the writing nozzle and pipe "Tartarus" (the pit beneath Hades!) onto a sheet of parchment paper. Let set. Spread the remaining chocolate thinly onto the strips of parchment paper. Cool until set, then break into shards and arrange around the cake. Place the "Tartarus" on top of the cake, then pipe the remaining ganache around the base.

The piping on this cake looks impressive but is actually easy to master—just keep your hand steady and take your time.

White Chocolate & Blueberry Cake

FOR THE SPONGE
¾ cup plus 2 Tbsp unsalted butter, softened
1 cup granulated sugar
1 tsp vanilla extract
4 large eggs
1¾ cups self-rising flour, sifted
1¼ cups blueberries
3½ oz white chocolate shavings, to decorate

FOR THE BUTTERCREAM
10 oz white chocolate chips
½ cup heavy cream
2 cups unsalted butter, softened
7¼ cups confectioners' sugar, sifted
¼ cup homemade or good-quality blueberry jam

YOU WILL NEED
8-inch round cake pans x 3, greased, then lined (base and sides) with parchment paper
large piping bag, fitted with a large closed star nozzle

1 Preheat the oven to 400°F.

2 Beat the butter, sugar, and vanilla in the bowl of a stand mixer fitted with the paddle attachment, on medium speed for 2 to 3 minutes, until the mixture is pale and creamy. With the mixer on low, add the eggs one at a time, beating well. Then gently mix in the flour, beating until just combined.

3 Using a spatula, gently fold in the blueberries, then divide the mixture equally among the pans. Bake the sponges for 20 to 25 minutes, until golden brown and a skewer inserted into the centers comes out clean. Let cool in the pans.

4 Make the buttercream: Melt the white chocolate chips and cream in a bowl set over a pot of simmering water, stirring occasionally. Remove from the heat and set aside to cool.

5 Beat the butter and confectioners' sugar in the bowl of a stand mixer fitted with the paddle attachment, on medium speed for 1 to 2 minutes, until fluffy. Reduce the speed to low and add the cooled, melted chocolate, mixing for 20 to 30 seconds, until fully combined. Reserve one third of the buttercream in a separate bowl.

6 To assemble, place one of the sponges, top-side down, on a cake plate. Spread with one quarter of the buttercream from the mixer bowl. Top with a second sponge, and spread with another quarter. Top with the remaining sponge, then use another quarter of the buttercream to create a crumb coat over the sides and top of the cake. Chill the cake for 30 minutes.

7 Use the final quarter of the buttercream to cover the side of the cake. Press the chocolate shavings around the side to cover.

8 Lightly stir the blueberry jam into the reserved buttercream to create a ripple effect. Spoon this into the piping bag. Beginning at the outside edge and working inward, pipe spirals of buttercream to look like roses all over the top of the cake.

You'll need only a tiny slice of Mary-Anne's cake (from Season 2) to feel satisfied. It's a brilliant option if you're feeding a crowd.

Chocolate & Orange Mousse Cake

Mary-Anne

FOR THE JOCONDE PASTE
7 Tbsp unsalted butter, softened
¾ cup confectioners' sugar, sifted
2 to 3 extra-large egg whites
¾ cup plus 2 Tbsp all-purpose flour, sifted
orange food-coloring gel

FOR THE JOCONDE
2⅓ cups ground almonds
1¾ cups confectioners' sugar, sifted
6 extra-large eggs
⅓ cup all-purpose flour, sifted
½ cup cocoa powder
4 to 5 extra-large egg whites
2 Tbsp granulated sugar
6 Tbsp clarified butter, melted

FOR THE MOUSSE
finely grated zest and juice of 1 unwaxed orange
1 tsp powdered gelatin
1¼ cups heavy cream
6 oz 54% dark chocolate, broken into pieces
2 extra-large eggs, separated

FOR THE GELÉE
1 Tbsp arrowroot powder
½ cup plus 2 Tbsp pulp-free orange juice

1 Heat the oven to 425°F.

2 For the joconde paste, beat the butter and confectioners' sugar in the bowl of a stand mixer fitted with the paddle attachment, on medium speed for 3 minutes, until fluffy. Gradually add the egg whites, beating continuously, until fully combined.

3 Fold in the flour, then mix in enough food coloring to create the desired orange shade. Spoon the mixture into the large piping bag fitted with the plain nozzle. Pipe the mixture onto the baking sheets in random swirls and chill for 10 minutes.

4 For the joconde, beat the almonds, confectioners' sugar, and eggs together in the bowl of a stand mixer fitted with the paddle attachment, on medium speed for 5 minutes, until light and fluffy. Add the flour and cocoa powder and mix until combined.

5 Place the egg whites in a large, clean, grease-free bowl and, using an electric hand mixer, whisk to soft peaks. Add the granulated sugar and continue whisking to stiff peaks. Using a metal spoon, gently fold the meringue mixture into the chocolate mixture. Mix a large spoonful of the sponge batter into the clarified butter, then fold this back into the sponge.

6 Remove the piped joconde paste from the fridge. Divide the sponge mixture equally between the two baking sheets, smoothing it level over the paste. Bake for 7 to 8 minutes, until the sponges are lightly browned. Cover each sponge with a sheet of parchment paper, then invert the baking sheets onto the work surface and peel off the paper to reveal the pattern. Let cool.

ingredients and recipe continue

TO DECORATE

zest of 1 unwaxed orange, cut
into thin strips
½ cup plus 2 Tbsp heavy cream

YOU WILL NEED

large piping bag fitted
with a ¼-inch plain nozzle
18 x 13-inch baking sheets x 2,
lined with parchment paper,
then brushed with
melted butter
2 sheets of parchment paper
10-inch round springform pan,
greased, then base-lined
with parchment paper
skewers or chopsticks
large piping bag fitted with
a large closed star nozzle

7 Using the springform pan as a guide, cut out two circles of sponge to fit inside. Place one circle in the base of the pan. Cut long strips of sponge about 2 inches wide and use these to line the sides of the pan, ensuring the pattern is facing outward, and there are no gaps. Set aside.

8 For the mousse, pour the orange juice into a small bowl and sprinkle with the gelatin. Set the mixture aside for 3 minutes, then set the bowl over a small pot of simmering water and stir gently to dissolve the gelatin. Whisk the cream to soft peaks.

9 Place the chocolate in a bowl set over a pot of gently simmering water, and stir gently until melted. Remove the bowl from the heat, then stir in the orange zest, egg yolks, and gelatin until well combined. Fold in the whipped cream.

10 Place the egg whites in a clean, grease-free bowl and, using an electric hand mixer, whisk to stiff (but not dry) peaks. Gently fold the egg whites into the chocolate mixture until well combined.

11 Pour the mousse into the sponge-lined pan and place the remaining circle of sponge on top. Press down to ensure it's flat. If necessary, trim the sponge around the side of the cake so that it's level with the top. Chill for at least 2 hours.

12 For the gelée, mix the arrowroot powder with 1 tablespoon of the orange juice, then stir it into the rest of the juice. Transfer the mixture to a pot and heat gently until it thickens and turns clear (4 to 5 minutes). Set aside to cool.

13 Carefully remove the cake from the pan and place it on a serving plate or cake stand. To make the orange curls for the decoration, wind the thin strips of orange zest around the skewers or chopsticks, then set aside. Pour the cooled gelée over the mousse cake, and return the cake to the fridge for 30 minutes to set.

14 Using an electric hand mixer, whisk the cream for the decoration to soft peaks and spoon it into the piping bag fitted with the star nozzle. Once the cake has set, pipe the cream around the top edge, then decorate with the orange curls.

Miranda's meringue cake from Season 1 is a hybrid celebration of the best of sweet baking: chocolate brownie, fluffy meringue, and copious amounts of berries and cream.

Miranda

Brownie Meringue Cake

FOR THE BROWNIE
7 oz 70% dark chocolate, roughly chopped
¾ cup plus 2 Tbsp unsalted butter, softened
2 cups confectioners' sugar, sifted
3 large eggs, beaten
¾ cup plus 2 Tbsp all-purpose flour, sifted

FOR THE MERINGUE TOPPING
4 large egg whites
¼ tsp cream of tartar
1 cup granulated sugar
⅔ cup roasted hazelnuts, chopped

FOR THE FILLING
1¼ cups heavy cream
¾ cup confectioners' sugar, sifted
2½ cups raspberries

TO DECORATE
1⅔ cups raspberries
⅔ cup roasted hazelnuts, chopped
¾ cup pistachios, chopped

YOU WILL NEED
8-inch round cake pans x 2, greased, then base-lined with parchment paper

1 Heat the oven to 375°F. For the brownie base, place 6¼ ounces of the chocolate in a bowl set over a pot of steaming water. Allow to melt, stirring frequently, until smooth. Remove from the heat and set aside to cool.

2 Beat the butter and confectioners' sugar in the bowl of a stand mixer fitted with the paddle attachment, until pale and fluffy. Gradually add the eggs, a little at the time, then beat in the flour, one third at a time, until the mixture is smooth. Beat in the cooled, melted chocolate.

3 Fold in the remaining ¾ ounce of chopped chocolate. Divide the mixture between the pans and level with an offset spatula. Bake for 8 minutes, until the mixture has started to form a crust.

4 While the mixture is baking, start the meringue topping: Pour the egg whites and cream of tartar into the bowl of a stand mixer fitted with the whisk attachment. Whisk to stiff peaks, then whisk in the sugar, one quarter at a time, to a smooth, glossy meringue. With the mixer on low, whisk in the hazelnuts.

5 Remove the cake pans from the oven and reduce the temperature to 325°F. Divide the meringue between the two pans, covering the brownie. Smooth the surface of one of the meringues and "peak" the surface of the other. Bake for 25 minutes, until the meringue is firm. Remove from the oven and let cool in the pans.

6 For the filling, using an electric hand mixer, whisk the cream to soft peaks, then add the confectioners' sugar and two thirds of the raspberries. Whisk briefly to a thick, pink cream. Gently fold in the remaining raspberries.

7 Loosen the brownies with a round-bladed knife. Turn out the brownie with the flat-topped meringue onto a plate, meringue-side down. Spread with the raspberry cream, then top with the second brownie, peaked meringue upward. Decorate with the raspberries, hazelnuts, and pistachios before serving.

Rahul's moist chocolate cake from Season 9 is surrounded by crunchy chocolate soil and decorated with a piped garden. Feel free to be creative with your garden design, if you like.

Edible Rock Garden Cake

Rahul

FOR THE SPONGE
1¼ cups cocoa powder, sifted
½ cup boiling water
2¾ cups plus 1 Tbsp dark
   brown sugar
¾ cup plus 2 Tbsp baking
   margarine or softened
   unsalted butter
6 large eggs
3 cups self-rising flour, sifted
2 tsp baking powder

FOR THE ITALIAN
MERINGUE BUTTERCREAM
1 cup granulated sugar
4 large egg whites
1 cup plus 2 Tbsp salted butter,
   diced
1 cup plus 2 Tbsp unsalted
   butter, diced
1 tsp orange extract
1 tsp vanilla extract
1 tsp lemon extract
green food-coloring gel
   or paste
red food-coloring gel or paste

FOR THE CHOCOLATE SOIL
½ cup granulated sugar
2½ oz 70% dark chocolate,
   roughly chopped

1 Heat the oven to 350°F.

2 Beat the cocoa and boiling water in the bowl of a stand mixer fitted with the paddle attachment, on medium speed to combine, then add the remaining sponge ingredients and mix until everything is fully incorporated.

3 Divide the mixture proportionately among the four pans. Bake for 25 to 30 minutes, or until a skewer inserted into the centers comes out clean. Cool in the pans for 5 minutes, then turn out onto a wire rack to cool completely.

4 Make the Italian meringue buttercream: Heat the granulated sugar and 7 tablespoons of water in a medium pot over medium heat to dissolve the sugar, then increase the heat and boil until the syrup reaches about 230°F on a candy thermometer.

5 Leave the syrup on the heat and whisk the egg whites in the clean, grease-free bowl of a stand mixer to soft peaks. Keep the mixer running and, when the sugar syrup has reached 250°F, remove the pot from the heat and slowly pour the syrup in a thin, steady stream into the egg whites. Whisk until the outside of the bowl is at room temperature and the meringue is very thick and glossy.

6 Then start adding cubes of salted and unsalted butter, whisking after each addition to make a smooth, thick buttercream. Add the orange, vanilla, and lemon extracts and mix thoroughly. Cover, and chill until firm.

7 Make chocolate soil: Heat 2 tablespoons of water and the sugar in a small pot over medium heat until the sugar dissolves. Increase the heat and boil the mixture until it turns golden around the edges (or reaches 275°F on a

ingredients and recipe continue

YOU WILL NEED
8-inch round cake pans x 2,
     greased and base-lined
     with parchment paper
6-inch round cake pans x 2,
     greased and base-lined
     with parchment paper
candy thermometer
plate lined with parchment
     paper
2 small disposable piping bags

candy thermometer). Stir in the chopped chocolate—it will immediately form clumps and crumbs. Tip this onto the lined plate and let cool.

8 To assemble, sandwich the two larger cakes with 3 tablespoons of the buttercream, spread evenly. Spread 1 tablespoon of buttercream on top.

9 Sandwich the two smaller cakes with about 2 tablespoons of buttercream and stack these on top of the larger cakes.

10 Place 6 tablespoons of buttercream in a small bowl and add green food coloring to make a leaf color. Place 4 tablespoons of plain buttercream in a second bowl and color this red.

11 Spread the remaining plain buttercream around the top and sides of the stacked cake.

12 Place the red and green buttercreams in separate, small disposable piping bags. Snip off the tip of the bag of red icing and make a V-shaped cut in the end of the bag of green icing.

13 Pipe green leaves around the sides of both cake layers and a few on the top, adding red dots to make flowers. Sprinkle the soil around the bottom of each cake layer and sprinkle a little on top. Store the cake in the refrigerator and serve within 2 days.

Rob's gâteau (Season 2), layered with rich mousse, could easily double up as a dessert. Use mini balloons to make the chocolate bowls.

Rob

Raspberry Chocolate Cake

FOR THE CHOCOLATE SPONGE
4 large eggs
½ cup plus 2 Tbsp granulated sugar
a pinch of salt
¼ cup unsalted butter, melted
¾ cup plus 2 Tbsp all-purpose flour
1 Tbsp cocoa powder

FOR THE PLAIN SPONGE
4 large eggs
½ cup plus 2 Tbsp granulated sugar
a pinch of salt
¼ cup unsalted butter, melted
1 cup all-purpose flour

FOR THE MOUSSE
7¾ oz 54% dark chocolate
6 Tbsp unsalted butter
6 large egg yolks
1 cup granulated sugar
4 large egg whites
¾ cup plus 2 Tbsp heavy cream

FOR THE GANACHE
¾ cup plus 2 Tbsp heavy cream
¼ cup light muscovado sugar
7 oz 70% dark chocolate, broken into pieces

FOR THE CHOCOLATE RECTANGLES
7 oz 70% dark chocolate
7 oz white chocolate

1 Heat the oven to 350°F. Place the eggs, sugar, and salt in a bowl set over a pot of barely simmering water. Using an electric hand mixer, whisk on high speed until the mixture is thick and mousse-like, and leaves a ribbon trail when you lift the whisk.

2 Remove the bowl from the heat and whisk for 2 to 3 minutes to cool the mixture slightly. Drizzle half the melted butter around the side of the mixture and sift in half the flour. Fold in with a large metal spoon, then drizzle in the remaining butter and sift in the remaining flour and the cocoa. Fold very gently until mixed. Carefully pour the mixture into one of the cake pans.

3 Repeat the method in steps 1 and 2 for the plain sponge (this time sifting in only flour and no cocoa powder).

4 Bake both sponges for 30 to 35 minutes, until firm and slightly shrinking away from the sides. Let cool in the pans for 5 minutes, then turn out onto a wire rack to cool completely.

5 For the mousse, melt the chocolate and butter together in a bowl set over a pot of simmering water. Remove the bowl from the heat and set aside. Whisk the egg yolks in the bowl of a stand mixer fitted with the whisk attachment until pale and creamy.

6 Dissolve the sugar with ½ cup plus 2 tablespoons of water in a small pot over low heat, swirling the pot occasionally, until boiling. Boil until the temperature reaches 248°F on a candy thermometer. Very slowly pour the syrup in a thin stream into the egg yolks, whisking continuously on high speed until the mixture leaves a ribbon trail when you lift the whisk.

7 In a clean, grease-free bowl, whisk the egg whites to soft peaks. In a separate bowl, whisk the cream to soft peaks. Gently fold the chocolate mixture into the egg and sugar mixture, then fold in the whipped cream, then the egg whites, until everything is fully combined. Chill until needed.

ingredients and recipe continue

FOR THE CHOCOLATE BOWLS
7 oz 70% dark chocolate
1⅔ cups raspberries
dark and white chocolate
    cigars, to decorate

YOU WILL NEED
9-inch round springform pans
    x 2, greased, then base-lined
    with parchment paper
candy thermometer
extra sheets of parchment
    paper
3 mini balloons

8 Cut each cooled cake in half horizontally. Wash one of the cake pans and re-line with parchment paper that comes 2 inches above the side of the pan. Place one plain sponge in the base of the pan, top with one third of the mousse, then place a chocolate sponge on top. Follow with another third of the mousse, then another plain sponge, the remaining chocolate mouse, and finish with the chocolate sponge. Chill for about 1 hour, to set.

9 For the ganache, heat the cream with the muscovado sugar in a medium pot until the sugar has dissolved (3 to 5 minutes). Boil for 1 minute, then let cool for 1 minute. Add the chocolate, set aside for 5 minutes, then stir until smooth.

10 Remove the cake from the fridge and pour half the ganache over the top, then return the cake to the fridge until the ganache has set (at least 5 minutes). Remove the cake from the pan, peel away the paper, and place on a cake plate or stand. Spread the sides of the cake with the remaining ganache.

11 For the chocolate rectangles, melt the dark and white chocolates in separate bowls set over pots of simmering water. On sheets of parchment paper, spread out the melted chocolate into two (one dark and one white) rectangles measuring about 14 x 6 inches. Chill for at least 15 minutes, to set.

12 Using a hot knife, cut the set chocolate into rectangles, each measuring about 4 x ¾ inch. Place the chocolate rectangles around the side of the cake, alternating in color.

13 For the chocolate bowls, blow up the three small balloons to about 4 inches in diameter and tie a knot in the top. Line a baking sheet with parchment paper. Melt the chocolate in a small bowl set over a pot of simmering water.

14 When the chocolate has melted, dip the balloons in, holding them by the knotted end so that the chocolate comes one third of the way up the inflated parts. Place the balloons onto the lined sheet, holding them for a few seconds so the chocolate pools around the base of the balloon a little to support them. Chill for 1 to 2 hours, until set, then snip the balloons and carefully peel the rubber away from the chocolate.

15 Fill the chocolate bowls with raspberries and place them on top of the cake. Decorate with the chocolate cigars.

CHAPTER THREE

Bakers' Favorites

HENRY, 20, DURHAM
ENGLISH STUDENT

Henry's love of baking was inspired by *The Great British Baking Show*—as a child he would walk past the tent every day on his way to and from school. Henry grew up in Ilford and is currently studying English literature at university. His housemates think he's completely bonkers when he's frequently up baking until 2 a.m. in an attempt to perfect an undoubtedly difficult bake. He's involved in a large number of clubs and societies at university, and both acts and plays music at university events, but he can always find time to whip up a showstopper.

JAMIE, 20, SURREY
PART-TIME WAITER

Jamie's grandma and parents taught him the baking basics, but it was after an episode of *The Great British Baking Show* inspired him to make a braided loaf that his baking aspirations really took hold. Born and raised in Surrey, Jamie is working as a part-time waiter in the lead-up to studying sports science at university. He happily takes on more technically difficult bakes, such as a croquembouche and croissants and has a fairly traditional approach to his flavors—although he likes to experiment with what he can find in the house.

ALICE, 28, LONDON
GEOGRAPHY TEACHER

Alice grew up in a seaside town in Essex. At 15, while recovering from a back operation for scoliosis and no longer able to play sports, she turned her hand to baking—and perfected the fruit pavlova while she was living in New Zealand in her early 20s. After returning to the UK, she trained to be a geography teacher. Now living in east London, she uses cakes in her lessons—demonstrating everything from coastal erosion to volcanic activity. She loves making highly decorative layered cakes and puff pastry. Her baking style is intricate and delicate, full of flavor and enthusiasm—and has to make people go "Wow!"

MICHAEL, 24,
STRATFORD-UPON-AVON
THEATER MANAGER/FITNESS INSTRUCTOR

Michael's mother taught him to bake, encouraging him to learn from old, handwritten recipes passed down from his mother's grandparents. He was born in Newcastle but considers himself Scottish as he moved to Scone in Scotland at age seven and studied in Edinburgh. In his baking, though, he is especially inspired by the flavors of his Indian heritage. He now works as a manager at a theater company in Stratford-upon-Avon. Michael has attempted pretty much every discipline in baking, but his strengths lie in cakes and pastry.

PHIL, 56, ESSEX
HGV TRUCK DRIVER

Phil was introduced to the joys of baking bread in his home economics class at school, but it wasn't until six years ago that he started to take baking seriously. He now bakes four or five times a week, frequently making focaccia, granary bread, and brioche, but also pastry (he likes the challenge of hot-water crust, puff, and choux). Phil grew up in Barking, training to be a driver at age 17. He now lives in Rainham, with his wife and two daughters. Working the early shifts means that Phil can spend the rest of his day preparing some of the meals and baking treats for his family and friends. He is passionate about motorbikes and always turns up for biking meetings with bakes. He has been working really hard on his decoration and piping techniques over the last year and now also loves to create really delicately decorated cakes.

AMELIA, 24, HALIFAX
FASHION DESIGNER

Amelia has been baking for 19 years—watching her mum and grandma creating beautiful cake decorations inspired her to start baking as a child. Born to a Caribbean father and British/half-Polish mother, Amelia grew up in Halifax and studied in Leeds and Leicester. She honed her baking skills while at university, baking for friends and college fund-raising events. Now living in London and working as a sportswear designer, Amelia draws on her northern roots to inspire her baking and believes that freshly farmed produce is essential for a satisfying bake. One of her proudest bakes is a snow leopard cake that she baked for her nephew's fifth birthday—a Madeira and a chocolate sponge with intricately designed tiger and snow-leopard faces.

DAN, 32, ROTHERHAM
SUPPORT WORKER

Dan is predominantly a self-taught baker but has fond memories of his mum showing him how to bake a Victoria sponge as a child and his army-chef dad coming to school to teach how to braid and bake bread. He got serious about baking at age 21 in a bid to impress his then girlfriend (now wife) with a themed birthday cake. Born in Worksop and raised in Rotherham, Dan lives just 20 minutes away from where he grew up, with wife Laura and their three dogs. Dan's favorite part of the baking process is decoration and he loves producing awe-inspiring bakes. He made his own wedding cake and says the thing he is most proud of making is a towering croquembouche.

DAVID, 36, LONDON
INTERNATIONAL
HEALTH ADVISER

David grew up in rural Yorkshire, where his mum (who baked all the time—the family never ate a store-bought loaf at home) inspired him to start baking. His passion was further developed by his travels to Malawi (among other places), where he learned to build an oven out of an oil drum and invented a cake that could steam-cook over a village fire. David studied art and design before switching to nursing. When he's not traveling the world for work, he lives in London and has lots of hobbies like cycling and ceramics. David's baking repertoire is broad, but his strengths lie in bread. He's not into fancy, colorful icings, but prefers robust flavors and good, solid bakes.

HELENA, 40, LEEDS
ONLINE PROJECT MANAGER

Helena spent much of her childhood watching her Spanish grandmother cook and bake, but it was only after moving to Las Vegas as part of an exchange program at school and living with a Mormon family that Helena really started baking. She was born in Ceuta (an independent Spanish city in north Africa), raised in Lanzarote, and educated in mainland Spain. While getting her degree, she moved to Leeds on an exchange, and then married her onetime lodger. They have a daughter. Helena likes to use American flavors, such as pumpkin, pecans, maple, and cinnamon, in her bakes. She also likes to use traditional Spanish flavors, including almond and paprika, as well as incorporating her passion for all things Halloween into her baking creations.

PRIYA, 34, LEICESTER MARKETING CONSULTANT

Priya's first foray into baking was at an after-school baking club at her elementary school. Then, seven years ago, when she was given a stand mixer as a wedding gift, she went "baking bonkers." She now bakes with such enthusiasm that she's been known to bake bread well into the night. A freelance marketing consultant and self-styled perfectionist, Priya lives in Leicester with her husband and two children, and is writing her first novel. She has recently experimented with vegan baking and loves tropical, fruity flavors. She'd love to travel on a worldwide sweet-and-savory tasting tour.

MICHELLE, 35, WALES PRINT SHOP ADMINISTRATOR

Michelle first fell in love with baking as a child watching her mother doing traditional baking at home. She grew up on a farm and now lives in the seaside town of Tenby with her husband and teenage son. Michelle bakes almost every other day—whether that's making a simple loaf to have for breakfast or something sweet to eat for dessert. She loves experimenting with flavor combinations and using seasonal vegetables from her own vegetable patch. Her bakes are precise and finessed, and created with an emphasis on good-quality local produce.

ROSIE, 28, SOMERSET VETERINARY SURGEON

Rosie's baking passions began at age five, when she was given a children's baking book. She grew up in Oxfordshire, studied at Cambridge, and now lives in Somerset with her childhood-sweetheart husband and many animals. When Rosie's not treating drunken hedgehogs, performing spleen surgery on dogs, or on call, she's baking to unwind and keep the staff nurses well fed. With a love of patisserie, a little box of mixed pastries is Rosie's "go-to" bake. Her baking is inspired by her rural surroundings, from the orchards next door to the fresh eggs laid by her ducks and chickens.

STEPH, 28, CHESTER SHOP ASSISTANT

Steph's granddad got her baking, with his love of homemade bread. She has been baking with a vengeance for the past three or so years. She is primarily self-taught and considers herself an "intermediate, still-learning" baker. Steph's passion for sports and wellness inspires her baking: she enjoys the challenge of making her bakes healthier in whatever ways she can—adding vegetables or fruit, lowering the refined sugar, and prioritizing more nutritious fats. Cookies are Steph's "go-to" bake, but her signature bake is a sourdough loaf using her starter, which she calls "Sammy."

Inspired by his wife's lemon drizzle, Phil road-tested his lime cake first at a bike-club quiz night. Over time, he has customized it further—baking it in a Bundt pan and adding the lime crunch.

Phil

Lime & Coconut Bundt Drizzle

FOR THE SPONGE
1 cup unsalted butter, softened
1 cup plus 3 Tbsp granulated
    sugar
4 large eggs, beaten
2 cups self-rising flour, sifted
⅔ cup unsweetened shredded
    coconut
finely grated zest and juice
    of 1 unwaxed lime

FOR THE LIME CRUNCH
finely grated zest of
    2 unwaxed limes
2 tsp granulated sugar

FOR THE DRIZZLE
3 Tbsp lime juice
3 Tbsp confectioners' sugar,
    sifted

FOR THE ICING
¾ cup confectioners' sugar,
    sifted
1 Tbsp lime juice

YOU WILL NEED
9-inch Bundt pan, well greased
sheet of parchment paper
small disposable piping bag

1 Heat the oven to 350°F.

2 Beat the butter and sugar in the bowl of a stand mixer fitted with the paddle attachment, on medium speed for 5 to 6 minutes, until pale and creamy. With the mixer on low speed, add the eggs, a little at a time, beating well after each addition.

3 Using a large metal spoon, fold in the flour, coconut, and lime zest and juice until just combined.

4 Spoon the mixture into the prepared pan and level the surface. Bake for 40 to 45 minutes, until golden brown and a skewer inserted into the center of the cake comes out clean.

5 While the cake is baking, make the lime crunch: Mix together the zest and sugar in a bowl, then transfer the mixture to a piece of parchment paper and set it aside to dry slightly.

6 Make the drizzle: Use a wooden spoon to combine the lime juice and confectioners' sugar in a small bowl, until smooth.

7 When the cake is ready, remove it from the oven, prick it all over with a skewer, and spoon half the drizzle mixture over the top. Allow the cake to cool for 10 minutes in the pan, then turn it out onto a wire rack. Drizzle the remaining lime and sugar mixture. Let cool completely.

8 Once the cake has cooled, make the icing: Place the confectioners' sugar in a bowl and add enough of the lime juice to make a thick, pourable icing. Spoon the icing into the piping bag, snip off the end, and drizzle the icing over the cake, allowing it to collect in the ridges of the Bundt.

9 Let the icing set slightly before sprinkling the cake with the lime crunch to finish.

This spiced cake is inspired by the golden streusel cake served at breakfast during Henry's childhood family holidays in Germany. You could replace the walnuts with toasted pecans, if you prefer.

Apple, Maple & Walnut Streusel Cake

Henry

FOR THE SPONGE
2¼ cups self-rising flour, sifted
½ tsp baking powder
1 Tbsp ground cinnamon
½ tsp ground cardamom
½ tsp ground ginger
½ cup plus 1 Tbsp cold unsalted butter, diced
⅔ cup light muscovado sugar
9 oz Granny Smith apples, peeled, cored, and cut into small dice
⅔ cup dried blueberries or golden raisins
3 large eggs
¼ cup heavy cream
seeds from 1 vanilla pod

FOR THE STREUSEL TOPPING
¼ cup all-purpose flour
6 Tbsp demerara sugar
½ tsp ground cinnamon
¼ cup cold unsalted butter, diced
1¼ cups walnuts, roughly chopped, plus ½ cup left whole, to decorate

FOR THE MAPLE FROSTING
3 Tbsp unsalted butter, softened
⅓ cup light muscovado sugar
1 tsp maple syrup
½ cup full-fat cream cheese

TO SERVE
1 cup crème fraîche
3 Tbsp honey
1 tsp cinnamon
½ tsp vanilla extract

YOU WILL NEED
8-inch round springform pan, greased, then base-lined
small piping bag fitted with a medium closed star nozzle

1 Preheat the oven to 350°F.

2 Place the flour, baking powder, and spices in a large bowl. Rub in the butter, using your fingertips, to a breadcrumb consistency. Stir in the sugar, apple, and blueberries or raisins until evenly distributed.

3 Using a balloon whisk, in a small bowl lightly whisk together the eggs, cream, and vanilla seeds, then stir into the sponge mixture until combined. Spoon the mixture into the prepared pan and level with the back of the spoon. Set aside.

4 For the streusel topping, place the flour, sugar, and cinnamon in a bowl. Rub in the butter, using your fingertips, to a breadcrumb consistency. Stir in the chopped walnuts until evenly distributed. Sprinkle the topping over the cake, making sure it is fairly level.

5 Bake the cake for 1 hour 10 minutes, until golden brown on top and a skewer inserted into the center comes out clean. Carefully loosen the edges of the cake, cool in the pan for 20 minutes, then transfer to a wire rack to cool completely.

6 For the maple frosting, beat the butter, sugar, and maple syrup together until fluffy, then beat in the cream cheese until smooth. Place the frosting in the small piping bag fitted with the star nozzle and pipe rosettes around the top edge of the cake, placing a whole walnut on top of each to finish.

7 Just before serving, in a small bowl, mix together the crème fraîche, honey, cinnamon, and vanilla until well combined. Serve the cake in slices, with the flavored crème fraîche alongside.

Dan's version of his mum's coffee cake is layered and topped with coffee-flavored cream cheese buttercream to balance out any bitterness, and then sprinkled with a sweet espresso brittle.

Dan

Layered Coffee Cake

FOR THE SPONGE
2 Tbsp instant espresso
1 Tbsp boiling water
1½ cups unsalted butter, softened
1¾ cups granulated sugar
6 extra-large eggs, beaten
1 Tbsp golden syrup or light corn syrup
3 cups self-rising flour
1 tsp baking powder

FOR THE ESPRESSO BRITTLE
1 tsp espresso-roasted coffee beans or instant espresso
¼ cup unsalted butter, softened
1 Tbsp glucose syrup
4 tsp whole milk
⅔ cup confectioners' sugar, sifted

FOR THE COFFEE & CREAM CHEESE BUTTERCREAM
1 Tbsp instant espresso
1 tsp boiling water
¾ cup plus 2 Tbsp unsalted butter, softened
¾ cup full-fat cream cheese
4 cups confectioners' sugar, sifted

1 Preheat the oven to 350°F. Dissolve the coffee in the boiling water and let cool.

2 Beat the butter and sugar in the bowl of a stand mixer fitted with the paddle attachment, on medium speed for about 5 minutes, until light and creamy. With the mixer on low speed, gradually add the eggs, beating well after each addition. Add the golden syrup or light corn syrup and prepared coffee and beat until combined.

3 Sift the flour and baking powder into the creamed mixture, then use a metal spoon to fold gently until incorporated.

4 Divide the mixture between the two prepared pans and bake for 30 to 35 minutes, until risen and a skewer inserted into the centers comes out clean. Cool in the pans for 5 minutes, then turn out onto a wire rack to cool completely. (Leave the oven on for the brittle.)

5 To make the brittle, if using coffee beans, place them in a resealable bag or sheet of folded parchment paper. Roll over them with a rolling pin to crush. Set aside.

6 Place the butter, glucose, and milk in a small pot over low heat and warm gently for 1 to 2 minutes, just until the butter has melted. Add the confectioners' sugar and stir until dissolved.

7 Increase the heat and boil, stirring, for about 4 minutes, until the mixture has reduced by about one third and is syrup-like and thick enough to coat the back of the spoon (it will look thick and frothy).

ingredients and recipe continue

YOU WILL NEED
8-inch round, deep cake pans
  or springform pans x 2,
  greased, then base-lined
  with parchment paper
9 x 13-inch baking pan, lined
  (base and sides) with
  parchment paper

8 Remove the syrup from the heat and allow it to settle to look like a thick custard. Then add the crushed coffee beans or instant espresso and stir until evenly distributed. Pour the mixture onto the lined baking pan and spread it out quickly and evenly so that it reaches the edges of the pan.

9 Bake the brittle for 12 to 15 minutes, until golden and caramel-like. It will look bubbly, but it will settle once it's out of the oven. Transfer the pan to a wire rack for the brittle to set.

10 To make the buttercream, dissolve the coffee in the boiling water and let cool.

11 Put the butter and cream cheese in a mixing bowl and beat with an electric hand mixer until smooth and combined. Gradually add the confectioners' sugar, a few tablespoons at a time, and beat with a wooden spoon for 2 to 3 minutes, until fluffy. Add the coffee and beat until combined.

12 Cut each cooled cake in half horizontally. Sandwich each cut cake with a generous amount of buttercream. Cover the top of one cake with another layer of buttercream, making sure to leave enough for a generous topping, then stack the other cake on top, giving you a four-tiered cake.

13 Top the cake with the remaining buttercream. Crush the brittle and sprinkle it over the top of the cake, to decorate. (You'll have more brittle than you need—try sprinkling it over your morning porridge, or over vanilla ice cream for a crunchy alternative to an affogato.)

This is Rosie's mum's chocolate beet cake. She makes it for all family birthdays, every year. It's a super-moist, super-easy bake that everyone loves!

Rosie

Chocolate Beet Cake

FOR THE SPONGE
¾ cup plus 2 Tbsp salted butter, diced
3½ oz 70% dark chocolate, broken into pieces
7 oz fresh, cooked beets, finely grated
1¾ cups self-rising flour, sifted
1 tsp baking powder
⅔ cup dark cocoa powder
1 cup plus 3 Tbsp dark brown sugar
4 extra-large eggs

FOR THE CHOCOLATE FUDGE FROSTING
⅔ cup condensed milk
½ tsp vanilla extract
3 Tbsp unsalted butter, diced
3½ oz 70% dark chocolate, chopped

YOU WILL NEED
7-inch round cake pans x 2, greased, then base-lined with parchment paper

1 Heat the oven to 350°F.

2 Place the butter in a medium pot over low heat and heat gently for about 1 minute, until melted. Remove the pot from the heat and add the chocolate. Let rest for 5 minutes, then stir until the chocolate has melted. Allow to cool for 10 minutes.

3 Place the beets in a large mixing bowl. Using a wooden spoon, stir in the flour, baking powder, cocoa, sugar, and eggs, then stir in the cooled butter and chocolate mixture until fully combined.

4 Divide the mixture between the two cake pans and bake for 30 to 35 minutes, until a skewer inserted into the centers comes out clean. Let cool in the pans for 5 minutes, then turn out onto a wire rack to cool completely.

5 To make the frosting, pour the condensed milk into a small pot with the vanilla and warm it over low heat for 1 to 2 minutes, stirring continuously to prevent burning, until the milk is hot but not boiling. Remove the pot from the heat and add the butter and chocolate. Let rest for 2 to 3 minutes, then stir until the butter and chocolate have melted and the mixture is smooth. Allow to cool until spreadable (about 1 hour).

6 When the frosting is ready, spread one sponge, top-side down, evenly with half the frosting. Stack the second sponge on top and spread with the remaining frosting to finish.

SERVES **HANDS-ON** **BAKE**

12 **30 MINS** **1 HOUR**

Amelia's recipe has evolved from her mum's much-loved carrot and apple muffins. Now a cake with cream cheese frosting, it is a favorite with her work friends and makes the house smell lovely!

Carrot & Apple Cake

Amelia

FOR THE SPONGE
2 large firm Granny Smith
   apples, peeled, cored, and
   grated
3½ oz carrots, peeled and
   grated
1¾ cups whole wheat flour
½ cup granulated sugar
2 tsp baking powder
1½ tsp ground cinnamon
1½ tsp ground ginger
¼ tsp salt
3 Tbsp honey
3 Tbsp maple syrup
⅔ cup vegetable oil
3 large eggs
1½ tsp vanilla extract
½ cup raisins
½ cup walnuts, chopped

FOR THE DECORATION
3 Tbsp unsalted butter,
   softened
¾ cup confectioners' sugar,
   sifted
3 Tbsp heavy cream
½ cup full-fat cream cheese
½ cup walnuts, finely chopped
a pinch of ground cinnamon

YOU WILL NEED
8-inch round, deep cake pan,
   greased, then base-lined
   with parchment paper

1 Heat the oven to 350°F.

2 Put all the sponge ingredients in a large bowl. Using a wooden spoon, beat them together to make a soft batter. Pour the mixture into the prepared pan and bake for 1 hour, until golden brown, risen, and a skewer inserted into the center comes out clean. Let cool in the pan for 10 minutes, then turn out onto a wire rack to cool completely.

3 To make the decoration, using an electric hand mixer, beat the butter in a bowl until really soft. Add the confectioners' sugar and beat on low speed until combined and smooth. Add the cream and beat again for about 4 minutes, until thickened, then add the cream cheese and beat again, briefly, until thick and creamy.

4 Spread the frosting over the top and sides of the cake and sprinkle the walnuts on top. Finally, dust lightly with the pinch of cinnamon.

Priya's cake is inspired by a work friend's recipe. Overripe bananas add their own natural sweetness, and the optional extras—in this case pecans—make this recipe very easy to adapt.

Priya

Banana & Pecan Loaf

FOR THE SPONGE
7 Tbsp unsalted butter, softened
½ cup demerara sugar
½ cup plus 2 Tbsp granulated sugar
2 extra-large eggs, beaten
2 to 3 overripe bananas (about 10½ oz peeled weight), mashed
2 cups all-purpose flour
1 tsp baking powder
½ tsp baking soda
½ tsp salt

FOR THE OPTIONAL EXTRAS
½ cup pecans, chopped, plus extra whole pecans for the top if you wish
½ cup walnuts, chopped, plus extra whole walnuts for the top if you wish
⅓ cup pitted dates, chopped

YOU WILL NEED
9 x 5-inch loaf pan, greased, then lined (base and sides) with parchment paper

1 Heat the oven to 350°F.

2 Beat the butter and both sugars in the bowl of a stand mixer fitted with the paddle attachment, on medium speed for about 5 minutes, until pale and creamy. Add the eggs, little by little, mixing well after each addition.

3 Mix in the mashed bananas, then sift the flour, baking powder, baking soda, and salt over the top. Fold them in using a large metal spoon.

4 Add any of the optional extras (pecans, walnuts and/or dates) you choose to make the cake your own, and stir them in until evenly distributed.

5 Pour the cake mixture into the prepared pan and add some nuts (if using) on top. Bake the cake for 1 hour, until golden, firm to the touch and a skewer inserted into the center comes out clean. Let cool in the pan for 5 minutes, then transfer to a wire rack to cool completely.

Helena's lemon meringue cake comes from her great-grandmother. Her family loves it so much that her siblings have to stake their claim straight after baking to ensure everyone gets their share!

Helena

Spanish Lemon Meringue Cake

9 oz graham crackers
½ cup unsalted butter, melted
5 large eggs, separated
1¾ cups condensed milk
juice of 5 lemons
6 Tbsp granulated sugar

YOU WILL NEED
8-inch round removeable
   bottom cake pan, greased,
   then lined (base and sides)
   with parchment paper

1 Heat the oven to 400°F.

2 Blitz the graham crackers in a food processor to fine crumbs. Remove 2 tablespoons of the crumbs and set aside. Add the melted butter to the crumbs in the food processor and blitz for a few seconds more until combined.

3 Transfer the graham cracker mixture to the prepared pan and use the back of a spoon to press it down firmly and evenly all the way to the edges of the pan to create an even base.

4 Place the egg yolks in a medium bowl. Using a balloon whisk, whisk in the condensed milk until fully incorporated. Then slowly whisk in the lemon juice until combined. Pour the mixture on top of the graham cracker base.

5 Place the egg whites in a clean, grease-free bowl and whisk with an electric hand mixer to stiff peaks. Whisk in the sugar, 1 tablespoon at a time, until the mixture forms a thick and glossy meringue. Spoon the meringue on top of the lemony layer in the pan.

6 Sprinkle the reserved graham cracker mixture on top of the meringue and bake the lemon meringue cake for about 25 minutes, until the top is golden brown. Let cool in the pan for 30 minutes, then transfer it to the fridge to cool completely.

7 When you're ready to serve, release the cake from the pan, remove the parchment paper, and serve in slices.

This is a recipe passed down from Steph's great-grandmother via her mum. A rich cake, soaked in brandy, it is best baked at least five weeks before eating. These quantities will also make a single 12-inch cake, baked for 4 to 4½ hours.

Great-Grandma's Christmas Fruitcake

Steph

FOR THE FRUIT CAKE
2 cups plus 2 Tbsp salted
   butter, softened
2½ cups dark muscovado sugar
8 large eggs, beaten
4¼ cups self-rising flour, sifted
1½ tsp pumpkin pie spice blend
¼ tsp nutmeg
a pinch of salt
3½ cups raisins
3½ cups currants
3½ cups golden raisins
¾ cup maraschino or red and
   green glacé cherries,
   quartered
1⅔ cups candied peel, chopped
1¾ oz candied angelica,
   chopped
finely grated zest of
   1½ unwaxed lemons
2 Tbsp brandy, plus extra
   for feeding the cake

FOR THE ALMOND PASTE
8⅓ cups ground almonds
2 cups granulated sugar
3¼ cups confectioners' sugar,
   sifted
2 Tbsp vanilla extract
juice of 2 lemons
3 large eggs, beaten
6 Tbsp homemade or
   good-quality apricot jam

1 Heat the oven to 300°F.

2 Beat the butter and sugar in the bowl of a stand mixer fitted with the paddle attachment, on medium speed for 5 minutes, until pale and creamy. With the mixer on low speed, add the eggs, a little at a time, beating well after each addition.

3 Place the flour, spices, salt, raisins, currants, golden raisins, cherries, candied peel, angelica, and lemon zest into a very large mixing bowl and stir together. Add the 2 tablespoons of brandy, then add the creamed mixture to the fruit and stir well with a large metal spoon until evenly combined.

4 Divide the mixture proportionately between the two pans. Level the tops, then bake: the 9-inch cake will take 3½ to 4 hours and the 6-inch will take about 2½ hours—or until the cakes feel firm to the touch, are a rich, golden brown, and a skewer inserted into the centers comes out clean. If they are coloring too much, cover them with foil for the remaining baking time.

5 Once the cakes are baked, let them cool completely in the pans, then transfer them to a plate or board, leaving the parchment paper attached to the sides and bottom to keep them moist. Don't worry if there's a little dip in the top of each cake.

6 Use a skewer to pierce the cakes all over, taking care not to pierce all the way to the bottom. Spoon 2 tablespoons of extra brandy into each cake, then cover the cakes with parchment paper and wrap them in foil. Place them in a tin or box, to store.

FOR THE ROYAL ICING
4 large egg whites
8 cups confectioners' sugar, sifted
4 tsp lemon juice
2 tsp glycerin

YOU WILL NEED
9-inch and 6-inch round, deep cake pans, greased then double lined (base and sides) with parchment paper, then double wrapped in strips of brown paper around the outsides of the pans (tie with string)

7 Uncover the cakes once a week for the next 4 weeks, each time feeding with 1 tablespoon of brandy each.

8 About 1 week before you intend to serve the cakes, make the almond paste. In a bowl, using a wooden spoon, mix together the almonds, granulated sugar, and confectioners' sugar. Add the vanilla, lemon juice, and enough of the beaten eggs to create a stiff paste (you may not need all the egg). Chill the paste for 30 minutes to firm up.

9 For the 6-inch cake you will need about one third of the paste; for the 9-inch cake the remaining two thirds. On a surface lightly dusted with confectioners' sugar, roll out one half of each weighed portion of almond paste to a circle large enough to cover the top of each cake and about ½ inch thick. With the remaining paste, roll out two long strips, one each to cover the sides of the cakes.

10 Heat the apricot jam in a small pot over low heat to loosen. Brush the top and sides of each cake with the warm jam, then place the appropriate circle of almond paste on top and wrap the appropriate strip around the side, trimming any excess and pressing the seam together where the pieces of paste meet. Loosely cover the cakes with parchment paper and let rest for at least 24 hours before adding the royal icing.

11 To make the royal icing, whisk the egg whites with an electric hand mixer for 1 to 2 minutes, until frothy. Whisk in the confectioners' sugar and stir in the lemon juice and glycerin. Whisk together until the icing is thick enough to hold stiff peaks.

12 Using an offset spatula, spread the tops and sides of the cakes with royal icing. Smooth it around the sides and rough up the tops to create a snow effect. Let the cakes rest overnight at room temperature to allow the icing to harden, then store in a tin or box until needed. (Don't wrap the cakes in plastic wrap or use a plastic container as they will go moldy.)

Inspired by the show, Michelle first made this cake five years ago for her husband's birthday—now it is a regular feature at family celebrations. She changes the jam flavor according to what's in season. Vanilla beans give a warming, spiced flavor to the custard.

Seasonal Prinsesstårta

Michelle

FOR THE VANILLA CUSTARD
1¼ cups whole milk
4 vanilla pods, seeds scraped from pods
3 extra-large egg yolks
¼ cup granulated sugar
¼ cup cornstarch
2 Tbsp unsalted butter

FOR THE BLACKBERRY & APPLE JAM
1⅓ cups blackberries
1 Braeburn or Fuji apple, peeled, cored, and grated
4 bay leaves
1½ cups granulated sugar
1 tsp pectin

FOR THE SPONGE
4 extra-large eggs
¾ cup granulated sugar
⅔ cup cornstarch, sifted
½ cup pus 2 Tbsp all-purpose flour, sifted
1 tsp baking powder
3 Tbsp unsalted butter, melted

FOR THE FILLING
2½ cups heavy cream

FOR THE MARZIPAN
2 cups ground almonds
6 Tbsp granulated sugar
1 cup confectioners' sugar, sifted
1 extra-large egg
1 tsp almond extract
purple food-coloring paste

1 For the custard, pour the milk into a pot with the vanilla seeds and pods and place over low heat for 2 to 3 minutes, until just simmering. Remove from the heat and set aside. In a large bowl, whisk the egg yolks, sugar, and cornstarch together until pale and creamy.

2 Strain the milk through a sieve and discard the vanilla pods. Stir the warm milk slowly into the egg mixture. Pour the mixture back into the pot and cook over low heat for 4 to 5 minutes, whisking, until the mixture thickens. (It should be very thick.) Remove the pot from the heat and beat in the butter until melted and incorporated. Transfer the custard to a bowl, cover the surface with plastic wrap to prevent a skin from forming, let cool, then place in the fridge to chill.

3 For the jam, tip the blackberries, apple, and bay leaves into a medium pot with the sugar and pectin. Cook gently over low heat, stirring occasionally, for 3 to 4 minutes, until the sugar has dissolved. Increase the heat and boil vigorously for about 4 minutes, or until the temperature reaches 219°F on a candy thermometer. Transfer the mixture to a heatproof bowl and let cool completely.

4 Heat the oven to 350°F.

5 Make the sponge: Whisk the eggs and sugar in the bowl of a stand mixer fitted with the whisk attachment, on high speed until thick and mousse-like, and the mixture leaves a ribbon trail when you lift the whisk.

6 Add the cornstarch, flour, and baking powder to the egg mixture and carefully fold in using a large metal spoon. Fold in the melted butter, taking care not to overmix.

ingredients and recipe continue

TO DECORATE
edible flowers or a sugarcraft
    flower garland

YOU WILL NEED
candy thermometer
9-inch springform pan,
    greased, then base-lined
    with parchment paper
medium piping bag fitted
    with a small plain nozzle

7 Pour the mixture into the prepared pan and bake for 25 to 30 minutes, until the sponge is golden and is just shrinking away from the sides. Cool in the pan for 5 to 10 minutes, then turn out onto a wire rack to cool completely.

8 To assemble the cake, using a serrated knife, cut the sponge horizontally into three even layers. Place one layer onto a serving plate. Remove the custard from the fridge and spread a very thin layer over the base of the first sponge.

9 Spoon one quarter of the remaining custard into the piping bag fitted with the plain nozzle and pipe a border around the edge of the sponge (as a "wall" for the jam). Spread about 5 tablespoons of jam over the sponge within the border. (You won't need all the jam—save the rest for spreading on toast.)

10 In a bowl, using an electric hand mixer, whip the cream for the filling until firm. Fold half the whipped cream into the remaining custard from the fridge. Spread one third of the custard cream over the jam. Place the second sponge on top and spread the remaining custard cream.

11 Place the third sponge on top. Spoon on the remaining whipped cream, covering the sides of the sponge and smoothing it into a small dome shape on the top. Chill the cake in the fridge for 1 hour.

12 Meanwhile, make the marzipan: Mix the ground almonds and sugars together in the bowl of a stand mixer fitted with the dough hook. Add the egg and almond extract and mix to a stiff dough (this will take seconds). Turn out the marzipan onto a surface dusted with confectioners' sugar. Using a toothpick, add a tiny amount of purple food coloring to the marzipan and knead it to an even color.

13 Roll out the marzipan on a surface lightly dusted with confectioners' sugar, into a circle (about 16 inches in diameter) large enough to cover the cake. Lift the marzipan up over the cake and shape it around the sides to get a smooth finish. Trim away any excess. Decorate with the edible or sugarcraft flowers.

Alice loves the combination of flavors in this cake—and the fact that you can easily double the recipe to add layers and make something extra-impressive for a special occasion.

Alice

Pear & Hazelnut Cake

1 Heat the oven to 350°F.

2 In a large mixing bowl, whisk together the sugar, eggs, and sunflower oil with a balloon whisk until smooth.

3 In a separate bowl, sift together the flour, baking powder, and cocoa powder. Add the pears, chocolate, and hazelnuts and toss together. Then, using a large metal spoon, fold the wet ingredients into the dry, until evenly combined.

4 Divide the mixture equally between the prepared pans and smooth the tops with the back of a spoon. Bake for 20 to 25 minutes, or until just firm to the touch. Let cool in the pans for 10 minutes, then turn out onto a wire rack to cool completely.

5 While the cakes are baking, make the poached pears: Pour 1⅔ cups of water into a medium pot. Place over medium heat and add the sugar, cinnamon, and vanilla. Bring the mixture to a boil, then gently lower the pear halves into the sugar syrup, making sure they are fully submerged. Simmer the pears in the syrup for 5 to 7 minutes, testing occasionally with the point of a knife, until they are tender. Remove the pear halves with a slotted spoon and set aside to cool.

6 For the maple cream cheese frosting, place the cream cheese and butter in a bowl and beat with a wooden spoon until very smooth. Gradually add the confectioners' sugar, beating well after each addition, until the mixture is smooth and thick. Then stir in the maple syrup.

7 Once the cakes have cooled, spread a thick layer of the frosting on each cake. Thinly slice the pears and arrange the best slices on one of the cakes in a spiral. Put all the trimmings on the other cake. Stack the cakes one on top of the other, with the layer with the spiral of pears on top.

FOR THE SPONGE
1 cup plus 3 Tbsp light muscovado sugar
4 large eggs
¾ cup plus 2 Tbsp sunflower oil
1⅔ cups all-purpose flour
2 tsp baking powder
⅔ cup cocoa powder
4 ripe pears, peeled, cored, and cut into small chunks
5¼ oz 70% dark chocolate, finely chopped
1 cup toasted hazelnuts, finely chopped

FOR THE POACHED PEARS
½ cup granulated sugar
1 tsp ground cinnamon
½ tsp vanilla extract
2 ripe pears, peeled, halved, and cored

FOR THE MAPLE CREAM CHEESE FROSTING
½ cup plus 1 Tbsp full-fat cream cheese
½ cup plus 1 Tbsp unsalted butter, softened
2 cups confectioners' sugar
1 tsp maple syrup

YOU WILL NEED
8-inch round cake pans x 2, greased, then base-lined with parchment paper

This is a family recipe that has been passed down to Michael from his great-grandmother via his grandmother and mum—in fact, it's one of the first cakes he and his mum ever baked together.

Michael

Sticky Gingerbread Loaf

FOR THE SPONGE
2 cups all-purpose flour
4 tsp ground ginger
½ cup plus 1 Tbsp whole milk
1 tsp baking soda
½ cup vegetable oil spread
½ cup dark muscovado sugar
5 Tbsp golden syrup or light
   corn syrup
5 Tbsp molasses
1 large egg

FOR THE ICING
1¼ cups confectioners' sugar,
   sifted
4 to 5 tsp lemon juice

YOU WILL NEED
9 x 5-inch loaf pan, greased,
   then lined (base and sides)
   with parchment paper

1 Heat the oven to 325°F.

2 Sift the flour and ginger together into a large mixing bowl and set aside. Measure 1 tablespoon of the milk into a small bowl and stir in the baking soda.

3 Pour the remaining milk, along with the spread, sugar, syrup, and molasses into a medium pot and place over medium heat for about 2 minutes, until the spread has melted.

4 Let the spread mixture cool for 5 minutes, then pour it into the bowl over the flour and ginger. Add the egg and the baking soda mixture, and beat with a wooden spoon to a smooth, thick batter.

5 Pour the batter into the prepared pan and bake for 50 to 60 minutes, or until a skewer inserted into the center comes out clean. Let cool in the pan for 5 minutes, then transfer to a wire rack to cool completely.

6 Mix the confectioners' sugar with enough lemon juice to make a thick pouring consistency. Once the cake is cool, drizzle the icing over the cake to finish.

SERVES **8** **HANDS-ON** **35** MINS **BAKE** **40** MINS

A few years ago, Jamie's grandma brought him a licorice birthday cake. He loved it so much, he decided to make his own. Keep the licorice icing fairly thick to stop it from running down the sides.

Licorice Sponge Cake

Jamie

FOR THE SPONGE
1⅓ cups unsalted butter
¾ cup granulated sugar
¾ cup light muscovado sugar
6 large eggs, beaten
2⅓ cups all-purpose flour, sifted
1 tsp baking powder
1½ Tbsp licorice extract
shavings of white chocolate, to decorate

FOR THE BUTTERCREAM
⅓ cup salted butter, softened
1¼ cups confectioners' sugar, sifted
⅓ cup cocoa powder

FOR THE LICORICE ICING
1¼ cups fondant sugar or confectioners' sugar
1 tsp licorice extract
black food-coloring gel

YOU WILL NEED
8-inch round cake pans x 2, greased, then base-lined with parchment paper

1 Heat the oven to 350°F.

2 Beat the butter and sugars in the bowl of a stand mixer fitted with the paddle attachment, on medium speed for 3 to 5 minutes, until pale and creamy. Add the eggs, little by little, beating well after each addition.

3 Using a metal spoon, fold in the flour, baking powder, and licorice extract until combined. Divide the mixture between the two prepared pans and bake for 35 to 40 minutes, until a skewer inserted into the centers comes out clean. Let cool in the pans for 5 minutes, then turn out onto a wire rack to cool completely.

4 Make the buttercream: Place the butter in a mixing bowl and beat with an electric hand mixer until fluffy. Gradually add the confectioners' sugar and cocoa powder, and beat until fully combined. Spread the buttercream on one of the cooled cakes and place the other cake on top.

5 To make the licorice icing, mix the confectioners' sugar with the licorice extract and enough water to make a thick, pouring consistency. Mix in the black food coloring to turn the icing completely black. Pour the icing over the top of the cake and decorate with white chocolate shavings to finish.

SERVES · HANDS-ON · BAKE

12 · **25** MINS · **35** MINS

This was David's favorite recipe when he was growing up—he's always been obsessed with the flavor of almonds. His mum packed the cake with poppy seeds, too, to make it that bit healthier.

Almond Poppy Seed Cake

David

FOR THE SPONGE
½ cup plus 2 Tbsp poppy seeds
⅔ cup whole milk
3 large eggs
¾ cup plus 2 Tbsp granulated
  sugar
½ cup light olive oil
1 Tbsp good-quality
  almond extract
1⅔ cups all-purpose flour,
  sifted
1 tsp baking powder
⅔ cup ground almonds

FOR THE ALMOND GLAZE
¾ cup confectioners' sugar,
  sifted
½ tsp good-quality
  almond extract
¼ cup sliced almonds

YOU WILL NEED
9-inch Bundt pan or ring
  mold, well greased

1 Heat the oven to 350°F.

2 Put the poppy seeds and milk into a pot over medium–high heat. As soon as the milk comes to a boil remove the pot from the heat and allow the mixture to cool.

3 In a medium bowl, mix the eggs and the sugar with an electric hand mixer for 3 to 4 minutes, until thick and creamy. Little by little, pour in the olive oil and then the almond extract, whisking after each addition, until combined.

4 Whisk in the flour, baking powder, and ground almonds, and finally the milk and poppy seed mixture, whisking until you have a thick batter.

5 Pour the batter into the prepared pan and bake for 30 to 35 minutes, or until a skewer inserted into the center of the cake comes out clean. Let cool in the pan for 5 minutes, then transfer to a wire rack to cool completely.

6 While the cake is cooling, make the glaze: Mix the confectioners' sugar and almond extract together with 1 to 2 tablespoons of water to create a thick, pouring consistency. Drizzle the icing over the cooled cake.

7 Toast the sliced almonds in a dry frying pan until lightly golden brown, then sprinkle them over the icing to finish.

CHAPTER FOUR

Fruit & Nut

This fruitcake is a keeper. Double-wrap it in parchment paper, then in foil, and store it for up to 3 months, feeding it with extra brandy to help it mature (it will also freeze for up to 6 months). Use the table on page 180 for alternative sizes.

Traditional Fruitcake

1 cup plus 2 Tbsp maraschino or natural-colored glacé cherries, rinsed and halved
1⅓ cups golden raisins
1¾ cups plus 3 Tbsp raisins
2 cups currants
1 cup mixed candied peel
⅔ cup unsalted butter, diced
¾ cup dark muscovado sugar
1⅓ cups all-purpose flour, sifted
½ tsp ground cinnamon
½ tsp ground ginger
¼ tsp ground nutmeg
a pinch of ground cloves
½ tsp pumpkin pie spice blend
3 large eggs, beaten
¾ cup brandy, plus ½ cup to pour (and extra to feed, if necessary)

YOU WILL NEED
8-inch round, deep cake pan, greased, then lined (base and sides) with parchment paper
extra parchment paper and foil, for wrapping

1 Heat the oven to 325°F.

2 Place the dried fruit and peel into a large bowl (big enough to hold the entire mixture, once the butter and flour are added, too) and stir with a large spoon until everything is evenly distributed.

3 Melt the butter and muscovado sugar in a nonstick pan over low heat for 2 to 3 minutes, stirring occasionally.

4 Stir the flour and spices into the fruit mixture, then add the warm butter and sugar mixture. Add the eggs and brandy, and stir again to combine. Spoon the mixture into the prepared pan and level it with the back of a spoon.

5 Bake the cake for 1 hour, then reduce the temperature to 275°F and bake for 1 hour more, or until a skewer inserted into the center comes out sticky (but not wet).

6 Remove the cake from the oven and pierce it all over with a skewer. Pour the additional brandy over the top and let the cake cool in the pan completely.

7 Once the cake is cold, remove it from the pan along with the lining parchment paper. Wrap the cake in the lining paper, another two layers of parchment paper, and then in foil. Store the cake in a box (not an airtight plastic container) for up to 3 months in a cool, dry place. Feed with brandy from time to time, if you like.

SCALING QUANTITIES
TRADITIONAL FRUITCAKE

All these versions of the traditional fruitcake will give you a delicious 2-inch-deep cake (either round or loaf)—except for the 9 x 13-inch baking pan, which will be a more bite-sized 1 inch deep and is perfect for snacking or lunchboxes.

	10-inch round, deep cake pan	**12-inch round, deep cake pan**	**9 x 5-inch loaf pan**	**9 x 13-inch baking pan**
maraschino or natural-colored glacé cherries, rinsed and halved	1¾ cups	2½ cups	¾ cup plus 1 Tbsp	1⅓ cups
golden raisins	2¼ cups	3 cups plus 2 Tbsp	1 cup	1⅔ cups
raisins	3 cups	4¼ cups	1⅓ cups	2¼ cups
currants	3 cups	4⅓ cups	1⅓ cups	2⅓ cups
mixed candied peel	1½ cups	2¼ cups	⅔ cup	1 cup plus 3 Tbsp
unsalted butter, diced	1 cup plus 2 Tbsp	1½ cups plus 2 Tbsp	½ cup plus 1 Tbsp	¾ cup plus 2 Tbsp
dark muscovado sugar	1⅓ cups	1¾ cups plus 2 Tbsp	⅔ cup	1 cup plus 2 Tbsp
all-purpose flour, sifted	2⅓ cups	3½ cups	1¼ cups	2¼ cups
ground cinnamon	1½ tsp	2 tsp	½ tsp	1 tsp
ground ginger	1½ tsp	2 tsp	½ tsp	1 tsp
ground nutmeg	½ tsp	1 tsp	¼ tsp	½ tsp
ground cloves	good pinch	good pinch	pinch	good pinch
pumpkin pie spice blend	1½ tsp	2 tsp	½ tsp	1 tsp
large eggs, beaten	5	7	2	4
brandy	1 cup plus 3 Tbsp	1⅔ cups	½ cup	¾ cup plus 2 Tbsp
Baking time @ 325°F	1 hour, then reduce oven to 275°F for 1 hour 15 to 20 mins	1 hour, then reduce oven to 275°F for 1 hour 30 to 40 mins (cover with parchment paper for the final 30 to 40 mins)	1 hour 15 mins	1 hour

Don't be put off by the longer baking and cooling times for this cake—it's really simple to make. Dusting the fruit in flour before folding it in helps to prevent the berries from sinking in the mixture.

Blackberry Pound Cake

FOR THE SPONGE
1 cup plus 2 Tbsp unsalted butter, softened at room temperature
2 cups plus 2 Tbsp granulated sugar
1 tsp vanilla extract
5 large eggs
¾ cup whole milk
2⅔ cups all-purpose flour, sifted, plus an extra 1 Tbsp for dusting
2 tsp baking powder
a pinch of salt
1½ cups blackberries

FOR THE TOPPING
1¼ cups Greek yogurt
1 Tbsp honey
⅔ cup blackberries, halved
edible flowers (optional)

YOU WILL NEED
9-inch deep, round cake pan, greased, then lined (base and sides) with parchment paper

1 Heat the oven to 350°F.

2 Beat the butter, sugar, and vanilla in the bowl of a stand mixer fitted with the paddle attachment, on medium speed for 2 to 3 minutes, until pale and creamy.

3 With the mixer on low speed, add the eggs, one at a time, beating well after each addition (don't worry if the mixture curdles slightly—it will come together when you add the flour).

4 Gradually add the milk and mix well to combine. Using a large metal spoon, fold the flour, baking powder, and salt into the mixture, until just combined.

5 Put the blackberries in a small plastic bag with the extra 1 tablespoon of flour and give them a shake to coat. Gently fold them into the cake mixture until evenly distributed.

6 Pour the mixture into the prepared pan and bake for 50 to 60 minutes, until golden brown and a skewer inserted into the center comes out clean. Turn out onto a wire rack and let cool completely (1 to 2 hours).

7 Meanwhile, make the topping: Using a wooden spoon, beat together the Greek yogurt and honey in a bowl, until smooth.

8 Once the cake is completely cool, spread the topping on top. Decorate with the halved blackberries and then dot with edible flowers, if using.

This cake, Edd's creation from Season 1, is light and airy—think dreamy gâteau rather than a more filling banana bread.

Caramel, Cinnamon & Banana Cake

Edd

FOR THE CARAMEL
1 cup granulated sugar
¾ cup plus 2 Tbsp heavy cream
1 Tbsp unsalted butter

FOR THE SPONGE
8 extra-large eggs
1⅓ cups plus 1 Tbsp light brown sugar
1⅔ cups all-purpose flour
3 Tbsp cornstarch
1 Tbsp ground cinnamon
½ tsp ground nutmeg
3 Tbsp unsalted butter, melted and cooled
6 walnuts halves, roughly chopped
6 dried banana chips, roughly chopped
1 small banana
2 Tbsp granulated sugar

FOR THE SYRUP
¼ cup granulated sugar
1½ Tbsp vanilla extract

FOR THE CARAMEL FROSTING
½ cup plus 2 Tbsp granulated sugar
3 extra-large egg whites, at room temperature
a pinch of cream of tartar
1 cup unsalted butter, at room temperature

1 For the caramel, tip the sugar into a heavy-bottomed pot and melt over medium-low heat. Increase the heat and cook until golden-amber (3 to 4 minutes). Remove from the heat and carefully add one third of the cream (take care as it will spit). Once the bubbling has subsided, whisk in the remaining cream, then stir in the butter until smooth and thick. Let cool in a shallow dish, then place in the fridge to chill.

2 Heat the oven to 350°F.

3 For the sponge, place the eggs and sugar in a bowl set over a pot of simmering water. Using an electric hand mixer, whisk to melt the sugar.

4 Transfer the mixture to a stand mixer fitted with the whisk attachment and whisk on high speed until the mixture is thick and mousse-like, and leaves a ribbon trail when you lift the whisk.

5 Sift together the flour, cornstarch, cinnamon, and nutmeg. Sift one third over the egg mixture and fold in with a large metal spoon. Repeat, folding in the remaining flour mixture one third at a time, until there is no trace of flour in the mixture.

6 Divide the mixture evenly among the three pans and bake for 15 minutes, until a skewer inserted into the centers comes out clean. Cool in the pans for 10 minutes, then turn out onto a wire rack to cool completely.

7 For the syrup, heat the sugar with ½ cup of water in a pot over low heat, stirring until the sugar has dissolved. Boil until reduced in volume by half (2 to 3 minutes). Remove from the heat and stir in the vanilla extract. Let cool.

ingredients and recipe continue

YOU WILL NEED
8-inch round cake pans x 3,
    greased, then base-lined
    with parchment paper
kitchen blowtorch
candy thermometer

8 For the caramel frosting, tip the sugar into a pot with 3 tablespoons of water and cook over medium heat until the syrup reaches 237°F on the candy thermometer.

9 Whisk together the egg whites and cream of tartar in the bowl of a stand mixer fitted with the whisk attachment, on high speed until they form stiff peaks. Whisking continuously, pour the syrup down the side of the bowl, then continue whisking for 3 to 5 minutes, until the mixture is cool enough not to melt the butter. Add the butter a little at a time, whisking well after each addition, to a thick, smooth, creamy frosting.

10 Still whisking continuously, add the cooled caramel one quarter at a time, until light and fluffy.

11 To assemble, brush the sponges with the cooled syrup. Place one of the sponges on a cake plate and spread with one quarter of the caramel frosting. Top with the second sponge and spread with another quarter of the caramel frosting. Top with the third sponge, then cover the top and sides of the cake with the remaining frosting.

12 Sprinkle the chopped walnuts and banana chips around the edge of the cake, then cut the banana into 8, 10, or 12 slices (depending on the size of the banana). Place the slices on a baking sheet and sprinkle with the sugar. Using the blowtorch, caramelize the sugar, then place the sticky banana slices on the cake to decorate.

Jo's chocolate and orange cupcakes (from Season 2) use a classic pairing, but it's also easy to give them an alternative flavor. Substitute chocolate, coffee, or vanilla for the orange syrup, if you prefer.

Jo

Chocolate & Orange Cupcakes

FOR THE CUPCAKES
1¾ oz 70% dark chocolate,
   broken into pieces
1 cup all-purpose flour, sifted
1 tsp baking powder
⅔ cup granulated sugar,
   plus 3 Tbsp for the syrup
3 Tbsp unsalted butter,
   softened and diced
1 extra-large egg
½ cup whole milk,
   at room temperature
1 unwaxed orange
chocolate shavings,
   to decorate

FOR THE BUTTERCREAM
¼ cup whole milk
1¾ oz white chocolate
½ cup plus 1 Tbsp unsalted
   butter, softened
4 cups confectioners' sugar,
   sifted

YOU WILL NEED
12-cup muffin tin,
   lined with paper liners
large piping bag fitted with
   a large closed star nozzle

1 Heat the oven to 350°F. Melt the chocolate in a bowl set over a pot of simmering water. Remove from the pan and stir until smooth, then let cool.

2 Tip the flour, baking powder, and ⅔ cup of the granulated sugar into a food processor and pulse to mix. Add the butter and process to a sandy texture. Mix the egg into the milk, then with the machine running, slowly add the mixture through the feed tube. Scrape down the sides, add the melted chocolate and run the machine until the mixture is thoroughly combined.

3 Divide the mixture equally among the cupcake liners, then bake for 15 to 20 minutes, or until just firm to the touch.

4 Meanwhile, grate the zest from half the orange and reserve for decoration. Cut a long strip of peel from the remaining half and reserve for the buttercream. Juice the orange into a bowl and mix in the remaining 3 tablespoons of granulated sugar until dissolved.

5 Pierce the hot cupcakes in several places with a toothpick. Spoon the orange syrup over the tops and let rest for 5 minutes to soak in, then cool the cupcakes on a wire rack.

6 For the buttercream, heat the milk in a small pot until just below boiling. Remove from the heat and add the orange peel. Allow to infuse until the milk is cold, then discard the peel. Melt the white chocolate in a bowl set over a pot of simmering water. Stir until smooth, then let cool.

7 Using an electric hand mixer, beat the butter in a bowl until creamy. Slowly beat in the confectioners' sugar and the cooled milk, then beat in the cooled, melted chocolate, until smooth.

8 Spoon the frosting into the large piping bag fitted with the star nozzle. Pipe the buttercream onto the cupcakes in swirls and top with orange zest and chocolate shavings.

A glorious celebration of summer, this cake is topped with edible flowers—feel free to choose your favorites. The gooseberry compote is best made the day before you intend to bake.

Gooseberry & Elderflower Cake

FOR THE GOOSEBERRY COMPOTE
1 lb 2 oz gooseberries, topped, tailed, and halved
½ cup granulated sugar
5 heads of elderflower (optional)

FOR THE SPONGE
8 extra-large eggs
2 cups plus 1 Tbsp unsalted butter, softened
2⅓ cups granulated sugar
3¾ cups plus 2 Tbsp self-rising cake flour, sifted
4 tsp baking powder
small, edible meadow flowers, with stems, to decorate

FOR THE ELDERFLOWER & ROSE SYRUP
1 cup granulated sugar
6 Tbsp elderflower & rose cordial

FOR THE ELDERFLOWER & ROSE BUTTERCREAM
1½ cups plus 1 Tbsp unsalted butter
¾ tsp salt
¾ tsp white vinegar
6 Tbsp elderflower & rose cordial
10¾ cups confectioners' sugar, sifted
½ cup plus 2 Tbsp heavy cream

1 For the gooseberry compote, place the gooseberries in a deep-sided pot with 3 tablespoons of water and the sugar. Tie the elderflowers (if using) in a small piece of muslin and add to the pot. Bring to a boil, reduce the heat, and simmer for 15 minutes, until the gooseberries are tender. Remove from the heat and carefully pour into a shallow container. Let cool, then chill to set.

2 For the sponges, heat the oven to 375°F. Beat all the sponge ingredients, except the flowers, in the bowl of a stand mixer fitted with the paddle attachment, on medium speed for 2 minutes, until smooth.

3 Measure about one quarter of the sponge mixture into each of the three 8-inch pans and divide the remaining mixture between the two 6-inch pans. Bake the 6-inch sponges for about 20 minutes and the 8-inch sponges for 25 to 30 minutes, until springy to the touch. Remove from the oven and let cool in the pans.

4 For the elderflower and rose syrup, tip the sugar into a pot. Add ¾ cup plus 2 tablespoons of water and bring to a boil over gentle heat, stirring to melt the sugar. Boil for 3 to 5 minutes, until reduced to a syrup consistency or the temperature on a candy thermometer reaches 230°F. Remove from the heat, stir in the cordial, and set aside to cool until warm.

5 Using a toothpick, poke small holes all over the sponges and spoon three quarters of the warm (but not hot) elderflower syrup over the tops. Let the sponges cool completely in the pans.

6 For the elderflower and rose buttercream, beat the butter, salt, vinegar, and cordial together in the bowl of a stand mixer fitted with the paddle attachment, on medium-low speed for 2 to 3 minutes, until smooth.

ingredients and recipe continue

Fruit & Nut **191**

YOU WILL NEED
8-inch round cake pans x 3,
    greased, then base-lined
6-inch round cake pans x 2,
    greased, then base-lined
candy thermometer (optional)
1 large piping bag fitted with
    a medium plain nozzle
8-inch cake drum
3 plastic cake dowels
6-inch cake card

7 On low speed, add half the confectioners' sugar, then add half the cream and beat for 3 minutes, until very smooth. Add in the remaining confectioners' sugar and the remaining cream and continue beating on low speed for 3 minutes, until very smooth but not aerated. Spoon one quarter of the buttercream into the large piping bag fitted with the medium plain nozzle, leaving the remaining buttercream in the bowl.

8 To assemble, trim the sponges level, if needed. Pipe a dot of buttercream onto the 8-inch cake drum and top with an 8-inch sponge. Brush the sponge with one fifth of the remaining syrup, then spread with one eighth of the buttercream. Pipe a line of buttercream around the edge of the sponge to act as a reservoir and fill with one third of the gooseberry compote.

9 Place the second 8-inch sponge on top and repeat as in Step 8. Top with the third 8-inch sponge, brush with syrup, then spread one eighth of the buttercream over the top. Space the dowels in a triangle formation in the middle of the cake, about 3 inches apart, and push down through the sponges. Trim the dowels flush with the top of the cake.

10 Pipe a dot of buttercream onto the 6-inch cake card and top with a 6-inch sponge. Brush the sponge with one fifth of the remaining syrup, then spread with one eighth of the buttercream. Pipe a line of buttercream around the edge of the sponge to act as a reservoir and fill with the remaining compote. Brush the underside of the remaining sponge with the leftover syrup and place, top-side up, on the gooseberry compote. Spread with one eighth of the buttercream.

11 Using the remaining buttercream in the piping bag, spread a thin layer of buttercream over the sides of the cakes and smooth off to form a crumb coat. Then, using the remaining buttercream in the bowl, repeat the crumb-coating process to create a semi-naked effect with small patches of sponge peeping through. (You can scrape off more or less buttercream, according to the effect you want to create.)

12 Chill the cake until ready to serve, then decorate with the edible flowers immediately before serving (the flowers can wilt quickly, so do this at the very last minute).

The filling of Beca's (Season 4) moist, zingy cake (think vibrant twist on a lemon drizzle) is made from cream and mascarpone, so store any uneaten cake in the fridge—it will keep for 2 to 3 days.

Beca

Grapefruit Sandwich Cake

FOR THE SPONGE
1 cup granulated sugar
1 cup vegetable oil spread
4 extra-large eggs
1¾ cups self-rising flour, sifted
¼ cup ground almonds
finely grated zest of 1 unwaxed
    grapefruit and juice of ½

FOR THE GRAPEFRUIT SYRUP
juice of 1½ grapefruits
6 Tbsp granulated sugar

FOR THE GRAPEFRUIT CURD
finely grated zest of
    ½ unwaxed grapefruit
juice of 1½ grapefruits
3 Tbsp unsalted butter
¼ cup granulated sugar
2 extra-large eggs, beaten

FOR THE CANDIED PEEL
peel (but no pith) of
    ½ unwaxed grapefruit,
    sliced into thin matchsticks
6 Tbsp granulated sugar, plus
    extra for sprinkling

FOR THE MASCARPONE CREAM
⅔ cup mascarpone
½ cup plus 2 Tbsp heavy cream
6 Tbsp confectioners' sugar

YOU WILL NEED
8-inch round cake pans x 2,
    greased, then base-lined
small piping bag fitted with
    a large writing nozzle
medium piping bag fitted
    with a medium plain nozzle

1 Heat the oven to 350°F. Beat the sugar, spread, eggs, flour, almonds, zest, and juice in the bowl of a stand mixer fitted with the paddle attachment, on medium speed for 2 minutes, until smooth. Divide the mixture equally between the two pans. Bake for 25 to 30 minutes, until springy and a skewer inserted into the centers comes out clean. Cool slightly in the pans while you make the syrup.

2 Place the juice and sugar in a medium pot and bring slowly to a boil, stirring occasionally until the sugar dissolves. Then boil for 5 minutes to thicken. Cool slightly, then using a toothpick, poke holes in the warm sponges and spoon on the syrup. Allow the soaked sponges to cool in the pans.

3 For the curd, put the zest, juice, butter, and sugar in a bowl set over a pot of simmering water. Stir occasionally, until the butter has melted, then whisk in the beaten eggs. Gently whisk the mixture for about 10 minutes, or until very thick. Pour into a shallow dish and let cool, then chill until set. Spoon one quarter of the cooled curd into the small piping bag.

4 For the candied peel, boil the peel in a large pot of water for 15 seconds, then drain. Return the peel to the pot with the sugar and 5 tablespoons of water. Boil for 8 to 10 minutes, then transfer the peel to a wire rack. Sprinkle with sugar.

5 For the mascarpone cream, whisk the mascarpone, cream, and confectioners' sugar together to stiff (but not too stiff) peaks. Spoon one quarter of the mixture into the medium piping bag.

6 To assemble, place one of the sponges on a cake plate or stand. Spread half of the remaining mascarpone cream onto the sponge. Spoon the grapefruit curd over the cream, then top with the other sponge. Spread the remaining mascarpone cream on top, then pipe blobs of the mascarpone cream around the edge. Pipe dots of curd over the mascarpone blobs, and decorate the center of the cake with the candied peel.

This classic is named for the French word for strawberry. Although the baking and assembly are relatively easy, you'll need about 2 hours to chill the components, so give yourself plenty of time.

Fraisier Cake

FOR THE GÉNOISE
4 large eggs
¾ cup granulated sugar
1⅓ cups self-rising flour
¼ cup unsalted butter, melted

FOR THE CRÈME PÂTISSIÈRE
2½ cups whole milk
2 tsp vanilla extract
4 large eggs, plus 2 large egg
    yolks
¾ cup plus 2 Tbsp granulated
    sugar
½ cup all-purpose flour, sifted
½ cup cornstarch, sifted
⅔ cup unsalted butter, diced

TO ASSEMBLE
4 cups strawberries
pink food-coloring paste
    (optional)
7 oz marzipan
3½ oz 70% dark chocolate,
    melted

YOU WILL NEED
9-inch springform pan,
    greased, then base-lined
    with parchment paper
strip of acetate, cut to
    fit the side of the pan
medium disposable piping bag
9-inch diameter circle of cut
    card (optional)
sheet of parchment paper

1 Heat the oven to 400°F.

2 To make the génoise, whisk together the eggs and sugar in the bowl of a stand mixer fitted with the whisk attachment, on high speed until very light, tripled in volume, and the mixture leaves a ribbon trail when you lift the whisk.

3 Sift two thirds of the flour onto the mixture, then gently fold in with a metal spoon. Add the remaining flour and continue to fold in gently, retaining as much air as possible, but incorporating all the flour. Gently fold in the melted butter.

4 Pour the mixture into the prepared pan and bake for 20 to 25 minutes, until the sponge is pale golden brown and shrinking away from the sides of the pan. Cool in the pan for 5 minutes, then turn out onto a wire rack to cool completely.

5 To make the crème pâtissière, bring the milk and vanilla just to a boil in a pot over medium heat. Meanwhile, in a separate bowl, whisk together the whole eggs, egg yolks, sugar, flour, and cornstarch until smooth and creamy.

6 Pour the milk onto the egg mixture, whisking continuously, then pour back into the pot and cook over low heat for 7 to 8 minutes, stirring continuously, until thickened to a piping consistency. Remove from the heat and stir in the butter.

7 Allow the mixture to cool slightly, then pour it into a bowl to cool completely. Press a layer of plastic wrap onto the surface, to prevent a skin from forming, then chill for 1 hour, to set.

8 When you're ready to assemble the cake, slice the cooled sponge in half horizontally to make two thin, equal layers.

recipe continues

9 Line the sides of the springform pan with the acetate. Place one sponge layer, cut side upward, in the pan. With the back of a spoon, gently squash the edges of the sponge to push it up against the acetate.

10 Choose 10 to 14 strawberries of the same height and size, hull, and cut them in half lengthwise. Arrange the strawberries cut sides facing outward around the edge of the sponge, pointed ends upward. Make sure the strawberries fit snugly.

11 Spoon the chilled crème pâtissière into the piping bag. Snip a ¾-inch hole in the end and pipe the crème all over the base to cover the sponge, carefully piping between the fruit to fill any gaps. Using an offset spatula, push the crème up against the acetate. Reserve the remainder in the piping bag.

12 Reserve 7 of the remaining strawberries to decorate, then hull and dice the rest and spread them evenly all over the layer of crème pâtissière. Pipe the remaining crème over the top of the berries and level it with the offset spatula.

13 Gently place the remaining sponge layer on top, cut side upward. Lightly press down to ensure the cake is firmly pressed against the acetate.

14 Knead a tiny amount of pink food coloring into the marzipan to achieve a pale pink color (you could leave the marzipan natural-colored if you prefer).

15 Roll out the marzipan on a surface lightly dusted with confectioners' sugar to a 9-inch circle and about ¼ inch thick, using the cake pan or the measured circle of card as a guide. Place the marzipan disk on top of the cake, then chill the cake for 30 to 45 minutes.

16 While the cake is chilling, dip the reserved strawberries into the melted dark chocolate and place them on the sheet of parchment paper to set.

17 Decorate the top of the cake with the dipped strawberries, then release the pan and carefully remove the acetate just before serving.

Frances's winning wedding cake from Season 4 is as enchanting now as it was then—a beautiful combination of flavored sponges, coated in lemony buttercream and decorated with flowers.

Frances

Midsummer Night's Dream Cake

FOR THE GINGER SPONGE
1¾ cups plus 1 Tbsp dark muscovado sugar
1½ cups salted butter
1 cup molasses
1 cup golden syrup or light corn syrup
4 extra-large eggs
3 cups whole milk
6 cups self-rising flour
1 Tbsp baking soda
4 Tbsp ground ginger
1 Tbsp pumpkin pie spice blend
14 oz rhubarb, chopped

FOR THE SUNSHINE SPONGE
½ cup light muscovado sugar
1 extra-large egg
5 Tbsp sunflower oil
¾ cup plus 2 Tbsp self-rising flour
1½ tsp ground cinnamon
½ tsp baking soda
3½ oz carrots, peeled and grated
finely grated zest of ½ unwaxed orange
3 Tbsp pistachios, chopped
2½ oz canned pineapple, drained and chopped
1¾ oz ripe apricots, chopped

1 Heat the oven to 375°F. Make the ginger sponge: In a large pot melt the sugar, butter, molasses, and golden syrup or light corn syrup together over very low heat, stirring occasionally, until the butter has melted and the sugar has dissolved. Remove from the heat and cool for 10 to 15 minutes.

2 In a bowl, whisk the eggs and milk together until smooth. In a separate very large bowl, sift the flour, baking soda, ground ginger, and pumpkin pie spice together. Stir the warm butter and sugar mixture into the flour mixture, then gradually add the egg mixture and stir together well.

3 Divide the mixture between the two prepared 9-inch pans, scatter the rhubarb pieces over the top and bake for 1 hour, until a skewer inserted into the centers comes out clean. Cool in the pans for 15 minutes, then turn out onto a wire rack to cool completely.

4 To make the sunshine sponge, mix the sugar, egg, and oil together in a bowl. In a separate bowl, sift the flour, cinnamon, and baking soda together.

5 Fold the flour mixture into the egg mixture, then fold in the carrots, orange zest, pistachios, pineapple, and apricots. Spoon the mixture into the prepared 4-inch cake pan and bake for about 40 minutes, until a skewer inserted into the center comes out clean. Cool in the pan for 15 minutes, then turn out onto a wire rack to cool completely.

6 To make the lemon sponge, beat the butter and sugar together in a bowl until pale and creamy. Gradually add the beaten eggs, a little at a time, beating well after each addition. If the mixture looks as if it might curdle, add a spoonful of the flour. Sift in the remaining flour and the ground almonds. Add the lemon zest and fold together.

ingredients and recipe continue

FOR THE LEMON SPONGE
1⅓ cups plus 2 Tbsp salted
 butter
1½ cups plus 2 Tbsp granulated
 sugar
5 extra-large eggs, beaten
2⅓ cups self-rising flour
⅔ cup ground almonds
finely grated zest of
 3 unwaxed lemons

FOR THE MARZIPAN BEES
½ egg, beaten
¼ tsp orange blossom
 honey, plus a little extra
finely grated zest of
 ¼ unwaxed orange
¼ tsp orange blossom water
¼ tsp vanilla extract
¼ tsp almond extract
½ cup confectioners' sugar
⅔ cup ground almonds
¼ oz 70% dark chocolate
about 36 sliced almonds
 (make sure they aren't
 chipped or broken)
edible gold leaf

**FOR THE LIMONCELLO
MERINGUE BUTTERCREAM**
3 cups granulated sugar
¾ cup plus 2 Tbsp lemon juice
10 extra-large egg whites
4½ cups unsalted butter,
 diced and softened
3 Tbsp limoncello
2 tsp lemon extract

FOR THE CREAM CHEESE FILLING
1¾ cups full-fat cream cheese
1⅔ cups confectioners' sugar,
 sifted

7 Divide the mixture equally among the three 6-inch cake pans and level the tops. Bake for 20 to 25 minutes, until a skewer inserted into the centers comes out clean. Cool in the pans for 5 minutes, then transfer to a wire rack to cool completely.

8 Make the marzipan for the bees. Whisk the egg, honey, orange zest, orange blossom water, and extracts together in a small bowl. Sift in the confectioners' sugar and ground almonds and stir to a smooth dough. Chill for 10 minutes to firm up.

9 Divide the mixture into 18 even-sized pieces. Roll each one in the palm of your hands and shape into the body of a bee. Set aside on a plate.

10 Melt the dark chocolate in a small heatproof bowl in the microwave, on a very low setting, checking every 10 seconds, making sure it doesn't overheat. Dip the fine paintbrush into the chocolate and paint three stripes onto each bee and put two dots at one end to make eyes.

11 Brush the ends of the sliced almonds with honey, then using the paintbrush to help you, carefully stick on a little gold leaf to each. Attach to the bodies to resemble wings. Set aside.

12 Make the buttercream (you may need to do this in two batches, using half the ingredients each time). Place 2½ cups sugar into a medium heavy-bottomed saucepan. Pour in the lemon juice and place over low heat, swirling the pan to dissolve the sugar completely. When the syrup has turned clear, increase the heat to medium and boil the syrup to 250°F on the candy thermometer.

13 Meanwhile, whisk the egg whites and the remaining ½ cup sugar in the bowl of a stand mixer fitted with the whisk attachment until it forms stiff peaks.

14 Pour the hot sugar syrup into the meringue in a thin, steady stream. Once the syrup is fully combined, whisk for 5 to 8 minutes more, until cool. With the mixer running, add the butter, a little at a time, then add the limoncello and lemon extract, until thick and creamy white. Set aside until ready to use.

FOR THE LEMON CAKE FILLING
4 to 5 cups raspberries

TO DECORATE
edible flowers
fresh fruit of your choice

YOU WILL NEED
9-inch round, deep cake pans x
    2, greased, then lined (base
    and sides) with parchment
    paper
4-inch round, deep cake pan,
    greased, then lined (base
    and sides) with parchment
    paper
6-inch round, deep cake pans
    x 3, greased, then lined (base
    and sides) with parchment
    paper
fine cake-decorating paintbrush
candy thermometer
11-inch cake drum
6-inch cake card
4-inch cake card
6 cake dowels

15 Make the cream cheese filling: Put the cream cheese into a large bowl with the confectioners' sugar. Fold everything together to fully combine and set aside in the fridge to chill.

16 Assemble the cakes: Remove the paper from all the sponges. Trim the ginger cakes to neaten. Spread a little bit of buttercream in the middle of the cake drum, then put one ginger sponge on top. Spread the cream cheese filling over the top of the cake and top with the other ginger sponge. Spread a thin layer of buttercream over the top and sides, then chill for 10 to 15 minutes.

17 Trim the lemon cakes to neaten. Spread a little buttercream onto the larger cake card, then top with a lemon sponge. Spread buttercream over the top of the cake, top with half the raspberries then layer up the other two cakes with buttercream and raspberries, finishing with a thin layer of buttercream on the top cake. Spread a thin layer of buttercream on the side. Lift onto a plate and chill for 10 to 15 minutes.

18 Trim the sunshine cake, put it on the smallest cake card, and spread a thin layer of the buttercream over the top and side. Chill the cake for 10 to 15 minutes.

19 Take the cakes out of the fridge. Cut three dowels to the height of the assembled ginger cake and push into the middle in a well-spaced triangle formation.

20 Cut the remaining three cake dowels to the height of the lemon cake and push them into the middle of the lemon cake, again in a well-spaced triangle formation.

21 Lift the lemon cake on top of the ginger cake and put the sunshine cake on top. Using an offset spatula, spread the remaining buttercream all over the cake, smoothing it out as you go. Decorate with the edible flowers, fresh fruit, and the bees.

Cakes don't come much more uplifting than this tropical fruitcake. It is packed with dried fruits for a natural sweetness that helps to keep down the refined sugar.

Sunshine Fruitcake

FOR THE SPONGE
2½ oz dried mango, diced
2½ oz dried papaya, diced
¾ cup dried apricots, chopped
⅓ cup golden raisins
1¾ oz dried pineapple, diced
1¼ cups tropical fruit juice
¾ cup unsalted butter, softened
¾ cup plus 2 Tbsp granulated
    sugar
3 extra-large eggs, beaten
1⅔ cups all-purpose flour
1 tsp baking powder
½ cup cornstarch
finely grated zest of
    1 unwaxed lime
⅓ cup blanched almonds,
    roughly chopped

FOR THE CANDIED PEEL
peeled zest of ½ unwaxed
    lemon, cut into matchsticks
peeled zest of ½ unwaxed lime,
    cut into matchsticks
¾ cup granulated sugar, plus
    3 Tbsp for dredging

FOR THE MARZIPAN FRUITS
1 cup confectioners' sugar,
    sifted, plus extra if necessary
1¼ cups ground almonds
1 extra-large egg yolk
½ tsp vanilla extract
yellow food-coloring paste
orange food-coloring paste
brown food-coloring paste
green food-coloring paste
purple food-coloring paste

1 Heat the oven to 325°F.

2 Place the mango, papaya, apricots, golden raisins, and pineapple in a bowl. Pour the tropical fruit juice into a pot and bring just to a boil. Pour the juice over the fruit and let cool to room temperature.

3 Beat the butter and sugar in the bowl of a stand mixer fitted with the paddle attachment, on medium speed for 3 to 5 minutes, until pale and creamy. Add the eggs, a little at a time, beating well after each addition.

4 In a separate bowl, sift together the flour, baking powder, and cornstarch, then fold the dry mixture into the wet mixture, along with the lime zest.

5 Drain the cooled fruit mixture, giving the sieve a good tap to remove any excess juice, then fold the mixture into the sponge batter until well combined. Spoon the sponge mixture into the prepared pan and sprinkle the chopped almonds on top. Bake for about 1 hour 15 minutes, until a skewer inserted in the center comes out clean. Let cool in the pan for 15 minutes, then transfer to a wire rack to cool completely.

6 For the candied peel, bring a small pot of water to a boil. Add the lemon and lime peel and boil for 5 minutes. Drain and return the peel to the pot. Add the sugar and ½ cup plus 2 tablespoons of water and place over low heat, stirring occasionally, until the sugar has melted. Simmer for 20 to 30 minutes, until translucent, then drain well and place the peel on a sheet of parchment paper. Dredge with the 3 tablespoons of sugar and set aside to dry.

ingredients and recipe continue

FOR THE TROPICAL ICING
¾ cup confectioners' sugar
1 to 2 Tbsp tropical fruit juice
pink food-coloring gel

FOR THE TOPPING
2 Tbsp blanched almonds,
    roughly chopped and toasted
3 Tbsp coconut flakes, toasted

YOU WILL NEED
9 x 5-inch loaf pan, greased,
    then lined (base and sides)
    with parchment paper
craft knife
cake-decorating paintbrush
cocktail umbrellas (optional)

7 For the marzipan fruits, beat together the confectioners' sugar, ground almonds, egg yolk, and vanilla in the bowl of a stand mixer fitted with the paddle attachment, on low speed until well combined. If the marzipan is too dry, add a little water; if it's too sticky, add extra confectioners' sugar.

8 Shape the marzipan into little fruits—2 oranges, 2 passion fruits, 2 bananas, and 2 pineapples—using food coloring and a craft knife to add color and detail. For example, try little crosses in the tops of the oranges with a little brown "stud"; purple, spherical passion fruits, halved and painted yellow inside with little black spots; brown lines painted down the lengths of the yellow bananas, joined at the top with a little brown stem; and scored diagonal lines on the yellow pineapples, with small green shoots for a top. Set aside.

9 For the tropical icing, sift the confectioners' sugar into a bowl and gradually add the fruit juice, mixing to a dropping consistency (you may not need all the juice). Add a tiny drop of pink food coloring to color the icing a very pale pink.

10 Drizzle the icing over the cake, then sprinkle the toasted almonds and coconut flakes for the topping. Decorate with the marzipan fruits, candied peel—and cocktail umbrellas, if you wish.

Liam's illusion masterpiece was a real highlight of Season 8 and would make a fantastic celebration showstopper for someone whose love of blueberry pancakes is equaled only by a love of delicious cake.

Stackin' Sunday Cake

Liam

FOR THE GRANOLA CRUMBLE
1½ cups pecans, roughly chopped, plus ½ cup extra for sprinkling
½ cup all-purpose flour, sifted
⅔ cup rolled oats
¼ cup wheat germ
1 tsp salt
7 Tbsp unsalted butter, chilled and diced
½ cup light muscovado sugar
¼ cup demerara sugar
⅔ cup raisins

FOR THE SPONGE
3 Tbsp buttermilk
1 tsp vanilla extract
1 overripe banana
2¼ cups self-rising flour
¾ tsp baking soda
½ tsp ground nutmeg
1 tsp ground cinnamon
¼ tsp salt
1 cup unsalted butter, softened
¾ cup plus 1 Tbsp granulated sugar
¼ cup light brown sugar
4 extra-large eggs, beaten

FOR THE SWISS MERINGUE BUTTERCREAM
4 extra-large egg whites
1⅓ cups plus 1 Tbsp light brown sugar
1¾ cups unsalted butter, diced, at room temperature
½ tsp vanilla extract
¼ cup Spanish forest honey

1 To make the granola crumble, tip the 1½ cups pecans into a food processor and blitz to a large crumb. Tip the flour into a separate bowl, add the blitzed pecans along with the rolled oats, wheat germ, salt, butter, and both sugars. Rub the butter in with your fingertips, until you have large chunks of crumble. Tip out onto the lined baking sheet and set aside.

2 Heat the oven to 350°F. To make the sponge, tip the buttermilk, vanilla, and banana into a food processor and blitz until smooth. In a separate bowl, sift the flour, baking soda, nutmeg, cinnamon, and salt together.

3 Cream the butter and sugar together in the bowl of a stand mixer fitted with the paddle attachment, on high speed for 4 to 5 minutes, until pale and creamy. Add the eggs, little by little, beating well after each addition. If the mixture begins to split, add 1 tablespoon of the flour mixture and beat again.

4 With the mixer on low speed, add the buttermilk mixture and the flour mixture, one third at a time, beating well after each addition, until combined. Divide equally among the three prepared pans and smooth with an offset spatula.

5 Bake the sponges and crumble mixture for 25 to 30 minutes, until a skewer inserted into the center of each sponge comes out clean and the crumble is deep golden brown. Remove from the oven and let the sponges cool in the pans for 15 minutes, then transfer to a wire rack to cool completely.

6 Allow the crumble to cool, then tip it into a food processor and pulse to a large crumb. Stir in the raisins and the ½ cup of pecans and set aside.

FOR THE BLUEBERRY COMPOTE
2⅓ cups frozen blueberries
2 Tbsp Spanish forest honey
4 tsp cornstarch

FOR THE FONDANT PANCAKES
1 lb white mini marshmallows
cream food-coloring gel
6⅔ cups confectioners' sugar,
    sifted
shortening, for greasing
cornstarch, for dusting
edible glue

TO DECORATE
cream food-coloring gel
golden yellow food-
    coloring gel
brown food-coloring gel
7 Tbsp vodka

FOR THE CREAM
1¼ cups heavy cream
confectioners' sugar, for
    dusting

YOU WILL NEED
baking sheet, lined
    with parchment paper
6-inch round cake pans x 3,
    greased, then lined
    (base and sides)
    with parchment paper
kitchen twine

7 To make the Swiss meringue buttercream, using an electric hand mixer, whisk the egg whites and sugar together in a bowl set over a pot of gently simmering water, until the sugar has dissolved. The egg whites should feel smooth, not gritty.

8 Transfer the hot mixture to the bowl of a stand mixer fitted with the whisk attachment and whisk on medium-high speed to a stiff meringue, then continue whisking until the bowl is completely cool to the touch. Add the butter, little by little, beating continuously to a smooth, fluffy frosting. Whisk in the vanilla and honey, then set aside.

9 To make the blueberry compote, tip the blueberries into a pot with the honey and ¼ cup of water and bring to a boil over medium heat. Mix the cornstarch with 3 tablespoons of water, add it to the blueberries, and bring back to a boil, stirring gently, so as not to break up the fruit, for 3 to 4 minutes, until thick and glossy. Remove from the heat and let cool.

10 To make the fondant for the pancakes, melt the marshmallows with 2½ tablespoons of water and a small amount of cream food coloring in a large bowl set over a pot of simmering water, stirring continuously.

11 Remove from the heat and, using a wooden spoon, stir in the confectioners' sugar, one quarter at a time, mixing well after each addition, until firm. On a surface greased with shortening, knead the fondant into a ball, then wrap it in plastic wrap and set aside.

12 To assemble the cake, level the sponges, then using a small amount of buttercream, stick one of the sponges onto a serving plate. Spread one third of the buttercream over the sponge and top with a good sprinkling of the crumble and one third of the compote. Top with another sponge.

13 Spread the second sponge with another third of the buttercream, another sprinkling of the crumble, and third of the compote, then top with the final sponge.

14 Use the remaining third of the buttercream to cover the top and sides of the cake. Smooth off the excess buttercream with an offset spatula to create a crumb coat. Chill for 1 hour, until firm.

recipe continues

15 Divide the fondant into 12 pieces. On a surface lightly dusted with cornstarch, roll ten of the pieces into thin sausages, long enough to wrap around the cake. (Use a piece of twine to measure the circumference of the cake and use it as guide when rolling the fondant lengths, if you like.)

16 Wrap one of the fondant lengths around the base of the cake, sticking it together at the ends with edible glue and pinching the join together. Repeat with the remaining nine lengths of fondant until you have ten rolls of fondant around the cake, stacked one on top of the other, resembling a stack of pancakes.

17 Knead the remaining two pieces of fondant together and roll them out to a circle large enough to cover the top of the cake—this is going to be the "pancake" that tops the stack. Place the circle on top of the cake.

18 Combine equal quantities of cream and egg-yellow food coloring and dilute them with 5 tablespoons of vodka (start with small amounts, then add until you get your desired shade—you want it quite a light, cooked-pancake color at this point). Paint the pancake "stack" with the coloring.

19 Combine equal quantities of cream, egg-yellow, and brown food coloring and dilute the mixture with the remaining 2 tablespoons of vodka, then paint the edges of the pancakes to add darker detail, as desired.

20 Whip the cream and confectioners' sugar together, then spoon the whipped cream over the top of the cake to represent the pancake topping, then sprinkle on another good helping of the crumble and one third of the compote. Dust with confectioners' sugar before serving. (Any leftover granola crumble will keep in an airtight container in the fridge for up to 1 week and is delicious sprinkled over yogurt or ice cream.)

Nancy made these individual chocolate and orange cakes in Season 5, reinventing a popular classic to create a delicate bake that would look stunning on a cake stand at high tea.

Mini Orange Cakes

Nancy

FOR THE CHOCOLATE PASTE
5¾ oz 54% dark chocolate
6 Tbsp golden syrup or light corn syrup
cocoa powder, for dusting

FOR THE JELLY
1 unwaxed orange
5 Tbsp granulated sugar
½ gelatin sheet
2 tsp orange liqueur

FOR THE SPONGE
¾ cup vegetable oil spread
¾ cup plus 2 Tbsp granulated sugar
3 extra-large eggs, beaten
1 tsp vanilla extract
1½ cups self-rising flour, sifted
1½ oz milk chocolate, broken into pieces

FOR THE ORANGE PASTILLES
4 strips of unwaxed orange peel (from the orange for the jelly)
¼ cup granulated sugar

FOR THE ORANGE BUTTERCREAM
⅓ cup unsalted butter, at room temperature
2 cups confectioners' sugar, sifted

1 For the chocolate paste, melt the chocolate in a bowl set over a pot of simmering water until it reaches 104°F on a candy thermometer. Melt the golden syrup or light corn syrup in a pot over low heat, until it reaches 104°F on the candy thermometer. Remove from the heat. Pour the syrup into the chocolate and stir vigorously until it comes together. Pour into a shallow bowl, let cool, then chill until firm enough to roll out.

2 For the jelly, using a sharp knife, carefully slice off the top and bottom of the orange. Slice the peel away from the flesh, then remove any remaining white pith. Reserve the peel for the pastilles. Segment the orange, retaining any juices. Finely chop the segments, again reserving any juice.

3 Place the orange segments and juice in a pot with 3 tablespoons of water and the sugar and bring to a boil. Reduce the heat and simmer for 20 minutes, until reduced in volume. Meanwhile soak the gelatin sheet in a bowl of water until soft.

4 Remove the pot from the heat and blitz the orange syrup with an immersion blender until smooth. Add the orange liqueur, then squeeze out the gelatin and stir it into the orange mixture. Transfer to a bowl, let cool, then chill to firm up. Once firm, spoon the gel into a medium piping bag fitted with a small plain nozzle and set aside.

5 Heat the oven to 350°F. For the sponge, whisk the spread and sugar together in the bowl of a stand mixer fitted with the whisk attachment on medium speed for 3 to 5 minutes, until very light and mousse-like. Add the beaten eggs, a little at a time, and the vanilla extract.

ingredients and recipe continue

YOU WILL NEED
candy thermometer
2 medium piping bags,
   each fitted with a small
   plain nozzle
12-cup mini-cake pan, greased
   with butter
medium plain nozzle
small piping bag fitted with
   a small writing nozzle
2-inch round cutter

6 Gently fold in the flour, retaining as much air in the mixture as possible. Divide the mixture equally among the mini-cake cups in the prepared pan and bake for 20 minutes, until springy to the touch and evenly golden. Cool in the pan for 5 minutes, then transfer to a wire rack to cool completely.

7 For the orange pastilles, bring a small pot of water to a boil. Add the strips of orange peel and boil for 5 minutes. Drain, then using the end of the medium plain nozzle, cut out 12 small circles of peel.

8 Tip the sugar into a small pot with 3 tablespoons of water and cook over low heat, stirring occasionally, until the sugar has melted. Add the orange circles, bring to a boil, and boil for 5 minutes, until the syrup has thickened. Remove from the heat and transfer the orange circles to a wire rack and let cool, reserving the syrup.

9 For the orange buttercream, beat the butter, confectioners' sugar and 3 tablespoons of the reserved orange syrup (from Step 8) in the bowl of a stand mixer fitted with the paddle attachment—first on low speed, then when the mixture comes together, on high speed for 3 to 4 minutes, until light and fluffy. Spoon the mixture into the remaining piping bag fitted with a small plain nozzle.

10 To assemble, level the tops of the sponges to make them equal in height, then slice each sponge in half horizontally. Pipe the buttercream in small blobs around the edge of the bottom layer of each sponge, then pipe the jelly inside the circle of buttercream. Cover with the sponge tops.

11 To decorate, melt the milk chocolate in a small bowl set over a pot of barely simmering water. Spoon into the small piping bag fitted with a small writing nozzle. Set aside.

12 Roll the chocolate paste out on a surface dusted with cocoa powder to $\frac{1}{16}$ inch thick. Using the 2-inch round cutter, cut out 12 disks. Paint the tops of the cake with the reserved sugar syrup, then stick on the disks.

13 Pipe two fine lines of milk chocolate across each chocolate disk and decorate each with an orange pastille.

Rhubarb and custard are the perfect combination of tart and sweet, but you could fill the centers of these little vanilla sponges with any rich fruits— just adjust the sugar accordingly.

Rhubarb & Custard Cupcakes

FOR THE RHUBARB FILLING
5¼ oz rhubarb, cut into
   large chunks
2 Tbsp granulated sugar
finely grated zest of
   ½ unwaxed orange

FOR THE CUPCAKES
7 Tbsp unsalted butter,
   softened
½ cup granulated sugar
1½ tsp vanilla extract
2 large eggs
¾ cup plus 2 Tbsp self-rising
   flour, sifted
1 Tbsp custard powder or
   cornstarch
½ tsp baking powder

FOR THE CRUMBLE TOPPING
1 Tbsp unsalted butter
¼ cup all-purpose flour
a pinch of salt
1 Tbsp granulated sugar
1 Tbsp light muscovado sugar

FOR THE BUTTERCREAM
½ cup plus 1 Tbsp unsalted
   butter, softened
2 cups confectioners' sugar,
   sifted
½ tsp vanilla extract
2 Tbsp custard powder
1 Tbsp boiling water

YOU WILL NEED
2 baking sheets
12-cup muffin tin lined
   with paper liners
apple corer
medium disposable piping bag

1 Heat the oven to 350°F. Spread out the rhubarb on a baking sheet and sprinkle with the sugar and orange zest. Cover with foil and bake for 20 minutes, until soft.

2 Beat the butter, sugar, and vanilla in the bowl of a stand mixer fitted with the paddle attachment, on medium speed for 5 minutes, until pale and creamy. Beat in the eggs, one at a time.

3 Mix the flour, custard powder, and baking powder together, then add to the mixture, one third at a time, until just combined. Spoon equally into the cupcake liners and bake for 15 to 20 minutes, until springy and golden. Place the tin on a wire rack for the cakes to cool completely.

4 While the cakes are cooling, blitz the cooled rhubarb and all its juices in a food processor to a smooth purée. Set aside.

5 To make the crumble topping, rub the butter into the flour, until the mixture resembles breadcrumbs. Add the salt and sugars, then spread the crumble in an even layer on a baking sheet. Bake for 10 to 15 minutes, until golden brown. Let cool.

6 Using an apple corer, cut out a small amount of the center of each cupcake and fill the hole with 1 to 2 small spoonfuls of rhubarb purée, reserving some of the purée for drizzling over the cakes.

7 Make the buttercream: Beat the butter in the bowl of a stand mixer fitted with the paddle attachment, on medium speed for 2 to 3 minutes, until soft. Add half the confectioners sugar, then the vanilla and custard powder, and finally the remaining' sugar and water, beating for 4 to 5 minutes on medium-high speed, until smooth and fluffy.

8 Spoon the buttercream into the piping bag and cut a ½-inch hole in the end. Pipe the buttercream onto each cupcake in a large dome. Drizzle with the reserved rhubarb purée, and sprinkle with crumble to finish.

SERVES	HANDS-ON	BAKE
30	**3** HOURS	**1¼** HOURS

Selasi created the original of this fabulous tiered cake, decorated with flavored buttercreams and edible flowers, in Season 7. It makes a formidable celebration cake that won't fail to impress.

Three-Tiered Floral Cake

Selasi

FOR THE CARROT SPONGE
4 cups self-rising flour
2 tsp baking powder
2 tsp ground cinnamon
2 tsp pumpkin pie spice blend
a pinch of salt
2 cups light muscovado sugar
1¼ cups walnuts, chopped
1 lb 1 oz carrots, grated
1 cup plus 1 Tbsp unsweetened
    shredded coconut
5¼ oz chopped fresh or well-
    drained canned pineapple
6 extra-large eggs, beaten
1¼ cups sunflower oil,
    plus extra for greasing

**FOR THE LEMON &
POPPY SEED SPONGE**
1 cup plus 2 Tbsp unsalted
    butter, softened
1¼ cups granulated sugar
4 extra-large eggs, beaten
2¼ cups self-rising flour, sifted
1 tsp lemon extract
¼ cup whole milk
¼ cup poppy seeds

**FOR THE VANILLA
& STRAWBERRY SPONGE**
1 cup plus 2 Tbsp unsalted
    butter, softened
1¼ cups granulated sugar
4 extra-large eggs, beaten
2¼ cups self-rising flour, sifted
1 tsp vanilla extract
¼ cup whole milk
¾ cup strawberries,
    hulled and chopped

1 Heat the oven to 350°F. For the carrot sponge, in a large mixing bowl, sift together the flour, baking powder, cinnamon, pumpkin pie spice, and salt. Stir in the sugar, breaking down any lumps, then the walnuts, carrots, coconut, and pineapple. Add the eggs and sunflower oil. Divide the mixture equally between the two 10-inch pans and bake for 25 to 30 minutes, until a skewer inserted into the centers comes out clean. Remove from the oven and cool in the pans.

2 For the lemon and poppy seed sponge, beat the butter and sugar in the bowl of a stand mixer fitted with the paddle attachment, on medium speed for 3 to 5 minutes, until pale and creamy. Add the eggs, little by little, beating well after each addition. Using a large metal spoon, fold in the flour, lemon extract, milk, and poppy seeds. Divide the mixture equally between the two 8-inch pans and bake for 20 to 25 minutes, until a skewer inserted into the centers comes out clean. Remove from the oven and cool in the pans.

3 For the vanilla and strawberry sponge, beat the butter and sugar in the bowl of a stand mixer fitted with the paddle attachment, on medium speed for 3 to 5 minutes, until pale and creamy. Add the eggs, little by little, beating well after each addition. Using a large metal spoon, fold in the flour, vanilla, milk, and strawberries. Divide the mixture equally between the two 6-inch pans and bake for 20 to 25 minutes, or until a skewer inserted into the centers comes out clean. Remove from the oven and cool in the pans.

4 To make the jam, crush the raspberries in a small pot, add the sugar and pectin, then bring to a boil over medium heat. Boil rapidly for about 10 minutes, until a candy thermometer reaches 221°F. Remove from the heat and cool completely.

5 For the lime and mascarpone buttercream, beat the butter and lime zest in the bowl of a stand mixer fitted with the paddle attachment, on medium speed for 3 to 5 minutes, until fluffy.

ingredients and recipe continue

FOR THE RASPBERRY JAM
1⅔ cups raspberries
1 cup granulated sugar
¾ tsp pectin

**FOR THE LIME & MASCARPONE
BUTTERCREAM**
¾ cup plus 2 Tbsp unsalted
    butter, softened
juice and finely grated zest
    of 1 unwaxed lime
6 cups confectioners' sugar, sifted
3 Tbsp mascarpone
pink food-coloring gel

**FOR THE VANILLA
CREAM CHEESE BUTTERCREAM**
¾ cup plus 2 Tbsp unsalted
    butter, softened
1 tsp vanilla extract
6 cups confectioners' sugar, sifted
¼ cup full-fat cream cheese
2 to 3 Tbsp skim milk
pink food-coloring gel

FOR THE LEMON BUTTERCREAM
½ cup unsalted butter, softened
finely grated zest of
    1 unwaxed lemon
3 cups confectioners' sugar
2 Tbsp lemon juice
2 to 3 Tbsp skim milk
yellow food-coloring gel

TO DECORATE
a selection of edible flowers

YOU WILL NEED
10-inch springform pans x 2,
    greased, then base-lined
8-inch springform pans x 2,
    greased, then base-lined
6-inch springform pans x 2,
    greased, then base-lined
candy thermometer
12-inch round cake drum
3 large piping bags, each fitted
    with a large closed star nozzle
6 cake dowels, 3 cut to the height
    of the large cake and 3 cut
    for the medium cake
8-inch cake card
6-inch cake card

Gradually add the confectioners' sugar and beat to combine. Mix in the mascarpone and lime juice, and the pink coloring to the desired dark pink.

6 For the vanilla buttercream, beat the butter and vanilla in the bowl of a stand mixer fitted with the paddle attachment, on medium speed for 3 to 5 minutes. Add the sugar and beat until well mixed. Beat in the cream cheese and the milk.

7 For the lemon buttercream, beat the butter and lemon zest in the bowl of a stand mixer fitted with the paddle attachment, as before. Gradually add the sugar. Beat in the lemon juice and milk, and the yellow coloring to the desired shade of yellow.

8 To assemble, spread a little lime buttercream on the cake drum. Sandwich the carrot cakes together with about 4 tablespoons of lime buttercream and place them on the drum. Using an offset spatula, spread a crumb coat of buttercream over the top and sides of the stacked cakes.

9 Place the remaining lime buttercream in a piping bag fitted with a star nozzle. Set aside. Position the three longest dowels in a triangle in the middle of the cake, pushing them all the way through so that they touch the cake drum.

10 Spread a little vanilla buttercream on the 8-inch cake card. On top, sandwich the lemon and poppy seed cakes with a little vanilla buttercream and cover with a crumb coat. Add pink coloring to the remaining vanilla buttercream to create a lighter pink shade. Spoon this into a piping bag and set aside. Position the shorter dowels in the cake in a triangle formation.

11 Spread a little lemon buttercream on the 6-inch cake card. On top, stack the vanilla and strawberry cakes using a little jam between each, and use a little lemon buttercream for a crumb coat. Place the remaining lemon buttercream in the remaining piping bag and set aside.

12 Chill all the cakes for 30 minutes to firm up, then stack the poppy seed cakes on top of the carrot cakes and the vanilla and strawberry cakes on top of the poppy seed cakes.

13 Pipe rosettes and stars of buttercream all over the cake, using the dark pink icing on the bottom tier, the lighter pink icing on the middle tier, and the yellow icing on top. Decorate with the edible flowers around each tier and on the top of the cake just before serving.

HOW TO...
FROST A SEMI-NAKED CAKE

Essentially, a semi-naked cake is a cake that has been crumb-coated. Naked cakes are bare or unfrosted on the sides, while a semi-naked cake has a very thin covering of buttercream frosting that allows the cake layers to peek through. Use the following instructions for creating semi-naked cakes or for crumb coating cakes you intend to go on to decorate fully.

You will need: cake-decorating turntable (optional) or cake stand or board; offset spatula; tall side scraper.

1 Assemble your layer cake as instructed in the recipe, spreading a generous layer of your chosen buttercream between the layers of cake and making sure the layers of sponge are even and flat. Fill and smooth any gaps at the side of the cake and between the layers to give your cake a far more finished and professional look at the end. Once you have a smooth surface, you're ready for the semi-naked coating.

2 Generously spread some additional buttercream around the sides of the cake with an offset spatula using gentle pressure and with one hand on top of the cake to secure it. Occasionally, revolve the turntable or cake stand or board while you work around the cake, to make sure it is evenly coated.

3 Once you have covered the side in a single coating of buttercream, spread an even layer over the top of the cake, spreading it out with the offset spatula.

4 Once the whole cake is covered, use a side scraper to smooth off any excess buttercream on the side, spreading and removing it until you are happy with the finish and coverage—expose some areas of the cake and leave others more covered.

5 Put the cake in the fridge to chill and firm up for at least 30 minutes and up to 1 hour. If chilling for more than 2 hours, cover loosely with plastic wrap after the first hour.

SEMI-NAKED CAKE DECORATING TIPS:

» Bake the cake as close to decorating as possible so the sponge is fresh. Let cool before decorating.

» To keep the sponge cake moist and prevent it from drying out, brush the cake with a simple sugar syrup. You could add coffee or even a liqueur to the syrup to give an extra flavor to your cake.

» Make sure the buttercream is the right consistency for spreading; it should have a light, fluffy, whippy texture.

» There may be a little buttercream crown around the top edge of your cake after you've smoothed the side. Using the offset spatula, smooth the buttercream crown inward, toward the middle of the cake, aiming to create sharp edges and a completely level top.

In Season 8, Sophie made this simple, tropical-tasting sandwich cake, topped with a pineapple flower made with baked pineapple "leather."

Pineapple & Coconut Sandwich Cake

Sophie

FOR THE SPONGE

1 pineapple, peeled, cut into three ¼-inch-thick rounds, then the remainder cored and cut into small chunks
¾ cup unsalted butter, softened
1 cup plus 2 Tbsp granulated sugar
5 extra-large eggs, beaten
2 cups plus 2 Tbsp self-rising flour, sifted
3½ oz fresh coconut chunks, peeled and blitzed to a gravel
3 Tbsp coconut flakes, toasted, to decorate

FOR THE COCONUT MERINGUE BUTTERCREAM

1½ cups granulated sugar
3 extra-large egg whites
1 cup plus 2 Tbsp unsalted butter, diced and softened
½ tsp coconut flavoring, plus extra to taste, if necessary

YOU WILL NEED

8-inch round cake pans x 2, greased, then base-lined with parchment paper
baking sheet lined with parchment paper
mini-muffin tin
candy thermometer
large piping bag fitted with a medium plain nozzle

1 Heat the oven to 350°F.

2 Weigh out 5¼ ounces (scant ⅔ cup) of the pineapple chunks for the cake mixture, drain thoroughly, and pat dry with paper towels. Then set aside 1¾ ounces (scant ¼ cup) for decoration (eat the rest).

3 Beat the butter and sugar in the bowl of a stand mixer fitted with the paddle attachment, on medium speed for 3 to 5 minutes, until pale and creamy. Gradually add the eggs, little by little, beating well after each addition. Add 1 tablespoon of the flour with the last three additions of egg, then sift in the remaining flour and fold to combine. Mix in the coconut "gravel" and pineapple chunks.

4 Divide the mixture equally between the prepared pans. Bake for 25 to 30 minutes, until a skewer inserted into the centers comes out clean. Cool in the pans for 2 minutes, then turn out onto a wire rack to cool completely. Reduce the oven to 275°F.

5 Prepare the pineapple flower: Put the 3 pineapple rounds on the lined baking sheet. Bake for 15 to 20 minutes, then turn over and bake for 15 to 20 minutes, until they are dry but flexible, with golden edges. Press each slice into a cup in the muffin tin. Return to the oven for another 20 minutes or so, until dry and golden. Cool in the tin, then stack the slices into each other to make a flower. Set aside.

6 Make the buttercream: Dissolve the sugar in 6 tablespoons of water in a medium pot over low heat (3 to 5 minutes).

7 While the sugar is dissolving, whisk the egg whites in the bowl of a stand mixer fitted with the whisk attachment to soft peaks. Once the sugar has completely dissolved, increase the heat to a rapid boil until the syrup reaches 250°F on a candy thermometer. Remove the pot from the heat.

recipe continues

8 With the mixer at full speed, pour the hot syrup onto the egg whites in a thin stream. Continue whisking until the meringue is very thick and glossy and has cooled to room temperature.

9 Gradually add the butter, whisking after each addition until the buttercream is smooth and thick. Incorporate the coconut flavoring, adding more to taste, if you prefer. Cover the bowl and chill until firm enough to pipe.

10 To assemble, place one sponge, top-side down, on a cake stand. Spoon the buttercream into the large piping bag fitted with the plain nozzle. Pipe large "kisses" on top of the sponge, saving half the buttercream for the next layer. Top with the second sponge, top-side upward, and pipe more kisses.

11 Place the pineapple flower in the center of the cake and decorate with toasted coconut flakes and the reserved 1¾ ounces of pineapple, chopped into ½-inch pieces.

CHAPTER FIVE

Free-From

*A classic cake adapted for vegan taste buds—
see the table on page 234 for the quantities
to make the cake in alternative sizes.*

Vegan Lemon Drizzle

FOR THE SPONGE
½ cup plus 2 Tbsp soy milk
1 Tbsp apple cider vinegar
1 tsp baking powder
¾ cup plus 2 Tbsp self-rising
  flour, sifted
1½ cups ground almonds
1½ vegetable shortening
½ cup plus 1 Tbsp granulated
  sugar
1 tsp vanilla extract
finely grated zest of
  1 unwaxed lemon
berries or edible flowers,
  to decorate (optional)

FOR THE DRIZZLE
juice of 1 lemon
2 Tbsp granulated sugar

FOR THE LEMON ICING
2 cups fondant sugar or
  confectioners' sugar, sifted
juice of 1½ lemons

YOU WILL NEED
9 x 5-inch loaf pan, greased,
  then lined (base and sides)
  with parchment paper

1 Heat the oven to 350°F.

2 Put the soy milk in a pitcher and add the vinegar. Let rest for 5 minutes to curdle slightly. In a bowl, stir together the baking powder, flour, and ground almonds.

3 Beat the shortening, sugar, vanilla, and lemon zest in the bowl of a stand mixer fitted with the paddle attachment, on medium speed for 3 to 4 minutes, until pale and creamy.

4 With the mixer on low speed, gradually add the curdled soy milk and beat for 30 to 60 seconds, until combined. Add the flour mixture, and mix on low until just incorporated.

5 Spoon the cake mixture into the loaf pan and bake for 1 hour, until the top is golden and a skewer inserted into the center comes out clean. Set aside in the pan to cool a little, while you make the drizzle.

6 Mix together the lemon juice and sugar in a small pitcher, until the sugar has dissolved. Pierce the still-warm cake all over with a toothpick and pour the drizzle over the top. Set aside in the pan and let cool completely.

7 To make the lemon icing, put the sugar in a bowl. Add the lemon juice, a little at a time, until you have a very thick but pourable icing. (You may not need all the juice.)

8 Once the cake has cooled, remove it from the pan and place it on a serving plate or stand. Using a spoon, drizzle or pour the icing over the top of the cake, allowing it to drip off the edges. Serve as it is, or decorate with berries or edible flowers (violas are lovely), if you wish.

SCALING QUANTITIES
VEGAN LEMON DRIZZLE CAKE

Use these quantities to adapt the recipe on page 232 for a 2-inch-deep, round 8-inch, 10-inch, or 12-inch cake pan, a larger loaf, and a rectangular baking pan.

	8-inch round, deep cake pan	10-inch round, deep cake pan	12-inch round, deep cake pan	9 x 5-inch loaf pan	9 x 13-inch baking pan
For the sponge					
soy milk	1¼ cups	1¾ cups plus 3 Tbsp	2¾ cups plus 1 Tbsp	1¼ cups	1½ cups
apple cider vinegar	2 Tbsp	3 Tbsp	4½ Tbsp	2 Tbsp	2½ Tbsp
self-rising flour, sifted	1¾ cups	2¾ cups	4 cups	1¾ cups	3½ cups
ground almonds	3 cups plus 2 Tbsp	4¾ cups	6¼ cups	3 cups plus 2 Tbsp	5½ cups
baking powder	2 tsp	1 Tbsp	1 Tbsp + 1 tsp	2 tsp	2½ tsp
granulated sugar	1 cup plus 2 Tbsp	1¾ cups	2½ cups	1 cup plus 2 Tbsp	2 cups plus 2 Tbsp
vegetable shortening	1 cup	1½ cups	2 cups plus 2 Tbsp	1 cup	1¾ cups
vanilla extract	2 tsp	2½ tsp	1 Tbsp	2 tsp	2 tsp
finely grated zest of...	2 lemons	3 lemons	4 lemons	2 lemons	3 lemons
For the drizzle					
juice of...	2 lemons	3 lemons	4 lemons	2 lemons	3 lemons
granulated sugar	2 Tbsp	3 Tbsp	4 Tbsp	2 Tbsp	3 Tbsp
For the lemon icing					
fondant sugar, or confectioners' sugar, sifted	1⅔ cups	2 cups plus 6 Tbsp	3¼ cups	1 cup	2 cups plus 6 Tbsp
juice of...	1 lemon	1½ lemons	2 lemons	½ lemon	1½ lemons
Baking time @ 350°F	1 hour	1 hour to 1 hour 10 mins	1 hour 15 mins	1 hour	45 mins

Suitable for vegans and delicious for everyone, this celebration cake was Briony's creation during Season 9. Aquafaba is the water from a can of chickpeas and behaves just like egg white.

Dairy-Free Hazelnut Mocha Cake

Briony

FOR THE SPONGE
5 cups self-rising flour, sifted
3 cups granulated sugar
1½ cups cocoa powder
1½ tsp baking powder
1½ tsp salt
1⅓ cups roasted hazelnuts, chopped
1 cup vegetable oil spread, melted
1⅔ cups hazelnut–flavored soy creamer
1 cup walnut oil
1 tsp xanthan gum
3½ Tbsp instant espresso
3 Tbsp boiling water

FOR THE MERINGUE KISSES
5 Tbsp aquafaba
½ cup granulated sugar
1 tsp xanthan gum
edible gold luster powder

FOR THE GANACHE
10½ oz vegan dark chocolate, broken into pieces
1¼ cups full-fat coconut cream
a pinch of salt
2 Tbsp coffee liqueur

FOR THE TRUFFLES
4½ oz vegan chocolate buttons
3 Tbsp full-fat coconut cream
¼ cup chopped roasted hazelnuts

1 Heat the oven to 350°F.

2 Make the sponge: In a large bowl, stir together the flour, sugar, cocoa, baking powder, salt, and hazelnuts.

3 In a medium bowl, using a balloon whisk, combine the melted spread, soy creamer, walnut oil, and xanthan gum. Dissolve the coffee in the boiling water, then whisk it into the bowl with the other wet ingredients.

4 Combine the wet and dry ingredients until smooth, then divide the batter equally among the three prepared pans. Bake for 30 to 35 minutes, until just firm and a skewer inserted into the centers comes out clean. Cool in the pans for 5 minutes, then turn out onto a wire rack to cool completely.

5 Make the meringues: Reduce the oven temperature to 225°F. Whisk the aquafaba in the bowl of a stand mixer fitted with the whisk attachment, on high speed for about 5 minutes, until doubled in size and thick and foamy.

6 With the mixer on low speed, add the sugar and xanthan gum, then increase the speed to maximum and whisk for about 10 minutes, until the mixture forms stiff peaks.

7 Place the meringue in the large piping bag fitted with a large star nozzle. Pipe "kisses" on the baking sheets (you'll have more meringue kisses than you need—you can freeze the spares once baked; or keep them in an airtight container for up to 1 week). Bake the meringues for 90 minutes, until dried out. Allow to cool, then dust with the gold luster powder.

8 Meanwhile, make the ganache: Place the chocolate in a heatproof bowl. Warm the coconut cream and salt in a pot

ingredients and recipe continue

FOR THE RASPBERRY JAM
2 cups raspberries
1¼ cups granulated sugar
1 tsp pectin
juice of ½ lemon

FOR THE ICING
¼ cup vegetable oil spread
1¼ cups confectioners' sugar,
    sifted
½ tsp vanilla extract
green food-coloring paste
red food-coloring paste

TO FINISH
2 Tbsp freeze-dried raspberries
¾ cup raspberries

YOU WILL NEED
9-inch round cake pans x 3,
    greased, then base-lined
    with parchment paper
large piping bag fitted with
    a large closed star nozzle
2 baking sheets lined with
    parchment paper
3-inch square, shallow
    container
melon baller
candy thermometer
small piping bag fitted with
    a small closed star nozzle
medium piping bag fitted with
    a large closed star nozzle
cake smoother

over low heat until it starts to bubble around the edges. Pour the coconut cream over the chocolate, let rest for 5 minutes, then mix until smooth. Stir in the coffee liqueur. Cover with plastic wrap and chill for about 2 hours, until set.

9 Make the truffles: Place the chocolate buttons in a heatproof bowl. Warm the coconut cream in a pot over low heat until it starts to bubble around the edges. Pour the coconut cream over the chocolate, let rest for 5 minutes, then mix until smooth. Pour into the square container and chill to set.

10 Put the chopped hazelnuts in a small bowl. When the truffle mixture has hardened, use the melon baller to scoop up 10 balls. Roll each ball in the hazelnuts to coat, then chill to set.

11 Make the jam: Cook the raspberries in a small pot over medium heat for 5 minutes, or until soft and pulpy. Reduce the heat to low, add the sugar, pectin, and lemon juice and heat gently until the sugar has dissolved. Increase the heat and simmer for about 5 minutes, or until the jam reaches 221°F on the candy thermometer. Transfer to a bowl and chill until needed.

12 Make the icing: Whisk the spread by hand until light and fluffy. Sift in half the sugar and whisk to combine, then whisk in the vanilla and the remaining sugar.

13 Put 2 tablespoons of the icing in a small bowl and add green food coloring until leaf-green. Place in the small piping bag fitted with the small star nozzle. Color the remaining icing red and place in the medium piping bag fitted with the large star nozzle. Set both aside.

14 Whisk the cooled ganache in the bowl of a stand mixer on medium speed until light and fluffy.

15 To assemble, cover the bottom sponge with a thin layer of ganache, then a thin layer of jam. Repeat for the next layer, then place the last sponge, top downward, on top. Spread the remaining ganache over the top and side of the layered cakes, then use a cake smoother to smooth the sides.

16 Pipe 3 or 4 large rosettes of red icing to make roses and use the green icing to pipe small rosettes representing leaves for each rose. Scatter dried raspberries over the cake and decorate as you wish with truffles, meringues, and fresh raspberries.

You can make the honeycomb for these cupcakes in advance, if you like—it will last for up to a week if it is well wrapped.

Dairy-Free Caramel Cupcakes

FOR THE CUPCAKES
⅔ cup light muscovado sugar
½ cup plus 2 Tbsp vegetable oil spread
½ tsp vanilla extract
2 large eggs
2 Tbsp dairy-free milk
1 cup plus 2 Tbsp self-rising flour, sifted
½ tsp baking powder

FOR THE CARAMEL
½ cup light muscovado sugar
½ cup plus 2 Tbsp coconut cream
2 Tbsp vegetable oil spread
½ tsp salt

FOR THE HONEYCOMB
½ cup granulated sugar
2 Tbsp honey
1 tsp baking soda

FOR THE BUTTERCREAM
½ cup vegetable oil spread
1⅔ cups confectioners' sugar, sifted
1 tsp vanilla extract
1 Tbsp caramel (optional)
1 tsp hot water, if necessary

YOU WILL NEED
12-cup muffin tin lined with 12 paper liners
8-inch square baking dish lined with parchment paper
apple corer
large piping bag fitted with a medium plain nozzle

1 Heat the oven to 350°F.

2 Beat all the cupcake ingredients together in the bowl of a stand mixer fitted with the paddle attachment, on medium speed for 3 to 4 minutes, until smooth and combined.

3 Spoon the mixture into the paper liners and bake for 15 to 20 minutes, until golden brown and just firm to the touch. Remove the cupcakes from the tin and place them on a wire rack to cool.

4 Place all the caramel ingredients in a small pot over medium heat. Bring to a boil and boil for 5 to 10 minutes, until reduced by half to a thick caramel. Pour into a bowl and cool for 10 to 15 minutes, then chill for 1 hour.

5 While the caramel chills, make the honeycomb: Heat the sugar and honey in a medium pot over low heat for 5 minutes, until the sugar has dissolved, then turn up the heat and boil for 4 to 5 minutes, until the mixture turns a golden caramel color. Remove from the heat and immediately whisk in the baking soda, taking care as the mixture will immediately foam up. Pour into the prepared baking dish and allow it to set for 30 to 45 minutes.

6 Meanwhile, make the buttercream: Beat the spread, sugar, and vanilla in a small bowl with an electric hand mixer until smooth and creamy. Add 1 tablespoon of the caramel, if you wish, and stir in to combine.

7 Using an apple corer, remove the center of each cupcake and fill the cavity with caramel.

8 Fill the piping bag with the buttercream. Pipe around the edge of each cupcake, working inward in a spiral to cover the top in a thick layer. Smash the honeycomb into chunks and place on top of the cupcakes.

Try to leave a few hours for this cheesecake to chill in the fridge before serving—it will help to really bring out the flavor in every layer.

Gluten-Free Berry Cheesecake

FOR THE COOKIES
½ cup vegetable oil spread
⅓ cup light muscovado sugar
1 tsp vanilla extract
1¼ cups gluten-free
    all-purpose flour, sifted
⅓ cup gluten-free rolled oats
⅓ cup unsweetened shredded
    coconut
a pinch of salt

FOR THE CHEESECAKE
¾ cup vegetable oil spread
3½ cups plus 1 Tbsp dairy-free
    cream cheese
¾ cup coconut yogurt
1 cup granulated sugar
1 tsp vanilla extract
3 large eggs, beaten

FOR THE BERRY COMPOTE
1 tsp cornstarch
1½ cups frozen blueberries
1⅔ cups frozen strawberries

YOU WILL NEED
large baking sheet, greased,
    then base-lined with
    parchment paper
9-inch springform pan,
    greased, then base-lined
    with parchment paper

1 Heat the oven to 400°F.

2 Make the cookies: Mix the spread and sugar together in a bowl with a wooden spoon. Stir in the vanilla and 2 tablespoons of water.

3 In a separate bowl, combine the remaining ingredients. Add them to the first bowl and bring together to a smooth dough. Roll out the dough on a lightly floured surface to about ¼ inch thick and cut into similar-sized pieces. (You don't need to be precise.) Transfer to the prepared baking sheet.

4 Bake for 15 to 20 minutes, until golden. Remove from the oven, then transfer to a wire rack to cool. Once cool, place the cookies in a freezer bag and bash with a rolling pin to a crumb.

5 Make the cheesecake: Beat the spread in a large bowl to soften. Stir in the cookie crumbs and tip into the pan. Press down evenly with the back of a spoon and chill the crust for 15 to 20 minutes to firm up.

6 Meanwhile, make the filling: Heat the oven to 400°F. Beat together the dairy-free cream cheese and coconut yogurt with a wooden spoon, until smooth. Add the sugar and mix until dissolved. Add the vanilla, then add the eggs, a little at a time, beating well after each addition. Pour the mixture over the crust, and bake for 1 to 1¼ hours, until golden. Set aside to cool (it may sink a little—that's okay).

7 Make the compote: Mix the cornstarch with 2 tablespoons of water to a paste. Put the blueberries and strawberries in a medium pot over low heat for 2 to 3 minutes, and bring to a simmer. Add the cornstarch mixture and mix well.

8 Increase the heat and bring to a boil, then reduce the heat and simmer for 2 to 3 minutes, until the fruit has softened but is still intact. Set aside to cool completely, then spoon onto the cheesecake. Chill for at least 2 hours before serving.

You could top this cake with a drizzle of fruit juice or maple syrup. Soak the fruit overnight, if you have time, for the best results.

Coconut Sugar Fruitcake

½ cup maraschino or glacé cherries
¾ cup plus 2 Tbsp golden raisins
¾ cup plus 2 Tbsp raisins
1½ cups hot, medium-strength black tea
2⅓ cups self-rising flour, sifted
1 cup coconut sugar
½ tsp ground ginger
1 tsp pumpkin pie spice blend
2 large eggs

YOU WILL NEED
9 x 5-inch loaf pan, greased, then lined (base and sides) with parchment paper

1 Place the cherries, golden raisins, and raisins in a bowl and pour in the hot tea. Set aside covered with plastic wrap and allow the fruit to soak for 6 to 8 hours, or ideally overnight.

2 Heat the oven to 350°F.

3 Put the flour, coconut sugar, ginger, and pumpkin pie spice in a large mixing bowl and stir to combine. Add the eggs and the soaked fruit (including any remaining soaking liquid) and mix until well combined.

4 Spoon the mixture into the prepared pan and bake for 1 hour, until a skewer inserted into the center comes out sticky (but not wet).

5 Allow the loaf to cool in the pan for 10 to 15 minutes, then transfer it to a wire rack to cool completely before slicing.

Once you master the ombre technique, you can turn any cake into a showstopper. Use any leftover buttercream to decorate cupcakes, and bake the sponges in batches if you don't have five pans.

Gluten-Free Lemon Ombre Cake

FOR THE SPONGE
2¼ cups unsalted butter, softened
2½ cups granulated sugar
finely grated zest of 2 unwaxed lemons
1 tsp vanilla extract
12 large eggs, beaten
3¼ cups gluten-free all-purpose flour, sifted
2 Tbsp baking powder
¾ tsp salt

FOR THE DRIZZLE
juice of 3 lemons
¾ cup granulated sugar

FOR THE BUTTERCREAM
5⅓ cups unsalted butter, softened
finely grated zest of 4 unwaxed lemons
1 Tbsp vanilla extract
19 cups confectioners' sugar, sifted
yellow food-coloring paste

YOU WILL NEED
8-inch round cake pans x 5, greased, then lined (base and sides) with parchment paper
8-inch round cake drum
10-inch round cake drum
cake-decorating turntable
large offset spatula
5 large disposable piping bags
tall side scraper

1 Heat the oven to 400°F.

2 Beat the butter, sugar, zest, and vanilla in the bowl of a stand mixer fitted with the paddle attachment, on medium speed for 1 to 2 minutes, until pale and creamy. Add the eggs, little by little, beating well after each addition.

3 Add the flour, baking powder, and salt one third at a time, mixing on low speed until incorporated.

4 Divide the mixture among the five pans and bake for 20 to 25 minutes, until springy to the touch and a skewer inserted into the centers comes out clean. Remove from the oven and let cool in the pans for 5 minutes, then turn out onto a wire rack to cool completely.

5 While the cakes are baking, make the drizzle: Put the lemon juice and sugar in a pot with 3 tablespoons of water, and place over medium heat for 2 to 3 minutes, stirring occasionally, until the sugar has dissolved. Remove from the heat, let cool, then brush a little drizzle over the sponges on the racks.

6 Make the buttercream: Beat the butter, zest, and vanilla in the bowl of a stand mixer fitted with the paddle attachment, on medium speed for 1 minute, until fluffy. Add the confectioners' sugar, one quarter at a time, starting on low speed, then increasing to high for 1 minute after each addition. Set aside.

7 Level the sponges and brush with a little more drizzle. Put a little buttercream on the 8-inch cake drum and top with the first sponge. Put the cake on the 10-inch drum, then on the turntable. Spread a tenth of the buttercream over the top of the cake, and over the edges a little.

recipe continues

8 Top with another sponge and repeat with another layer of buttercream. Repeat with another two sponges, then top with the final sponge, placing it cut-side downward.

9 Spread one tenth of the remaining buttercream all around the sides of the cake to create a crumb coat. Use another tenth of the buttercream to spread a thin, even layer over the top of the cake.

10 Using the offset spatula, smooth off the excess buttercream until the sides are smooth and neat. Remove the cake from the turntable and chill for 1 hour.

11 For the ombre layer, divide the remaining buttercream into five separate bowls. Using the yellow food coloring, tint the buttercream in four of the bowls a different shade of yellow, from bright to pale. Place each shade (including the plain) into a disposable piping bag. Place the cake back on the turntable.

12 Snip a ½-inch hole in the end of each piping bag. Starting with the brightest shade of yellow, pipe in circles around the bottom of the cake, making two or three rings up the side of the cake, so that you cover about a fifth of the height of the cake.

13 Repeat for the remaining shades, getting lighter each time, then use the plain buttercream just for the uppermost edge and the top of the cake, piping around the top edge and roughly filling in the top surface of the cake. Using the offset spatula, smooth the buttercream over the top of the cake.

14 Using a tall side scraper, swoop all around the cake to create an ombre effect. Hold the scraper edge against the cake, with the flat side of the scraper at a 45-degree angle to the side of the cake. In one confident motion, spin the turntable while sweeping the buttercream. Once you get back to your starting point, remove the scraper in a swift motion.

15 Using a sharp knife, gently remove any excess buttercream that has popped up on top of the cake. If you need or want to neaten your finish, go around once (but only once) more with a clean scraper. Place the cake back in the fridge to firm up.

16 To serve, use an offset spatula to lift the whole cake off the 10-inch drum and onto a cake stand or serving plate.

These gluten-free brownies are made with ground almonds instead of flour. Keep the raspberries whole when adding them to the mixture to create juicy pockets of deliciousness.

Gluten-Free Chocolate Berry Brownies

9¼ oz 70% dark chocolate, broken into pieces
½ cup plus 1 Tbsp unsalted butter, diced
1 tsp vanilla extract
1⅓ cups light muscovado sugar
4 large eggs, beaten
¾ cup cocoa powder
2¾ cups ground almonds
1¼ cups raspberries
⅓ cup sliced almonds

YOU WILL NEED
8½-inch square cake pan, greased and lined (base and sides) with parchment paper

1 Heat the oven to 400°F.

2 Melt the chocolate, butter, vanilla, and sugar in a bowl set over a pot of simmering water, stirring occasionally, for 5 minutes. Remove the bowl from the pot, add the eggs, and stir until fully incorporated.

3 Using a metal spoon, gently fold in the cocoa powder and ground almonds, then carefully mix in the raspberries—be gentle so as not to squash them.

4 Pour the brownie mixture into the prepared pan and sprinkle on the sliced almonds.

5 Bake the brownie mixture for about 30 minutes, until a skewer inserted into the center comes out sticky (but not wet). Allow the brownie to cool completely in the pan before cutting into 16 squares.

The blush pink rhubarb in the almond-rich polenta sponge looks stunning, and this fruity cake is immensely comforting—like a hug in a cake.

Gluten-Free Rhubarb & Polenta Cake

1 cup granulated sugar
⅔ cup unsalted butter, softened
1 tsp vanilla extract
finely grated zest of
    1 unwaxed orange
3 large eggs, beaten
¾ cup plus 3 Tbsp polenta
1½ tsp baking powder
1 cup ground almonds
14 oz rhubarb, trimmed and
    thickly sliced
sliced almonds, to decorate
confectioners' sugar, for
    dusting

YOU WILL NEED
8-inch round, deep,
    removable-bottom cake pan,
    greased, then lined (base and
    sides) with parchment paper

1 Heat the oven to 350°F.

2 Beat the sugar, butter, and vanilla in the bowl of a stand mixer fitted with the paddle attachment, on medium speed for 2 to 3 minutes, until pale and creamy. Reduce the speed to low, then add the orange zest. Add the eggs, little by little, beating well after each addition, until combined.

3 Fold in the polenta, baking powder, and ground almonds, mixing to a dropping consistency. Spoon half the mixture into the prepared pan. Level with an offset spatula.

4 Reserve a few pieces of rhubarb for decoration, then arrange the remaining rhubarb over the cake mixture in the pan. Top with the remaining mixture, spreading it out evenly, and decorate with the reserved rhubarb pieces.

5 Bake the sponge for 1 to 1¼ hours, until well risen and golden and a skewer inserted into the center comes out clean. Allow to cool for 1 to 2 hours, then turn out and place the cake, top-side upward, on a cake plate. Scatter a few flaked almonds over the top and dust with confectioners' sugar, to decorate.

The doneness test for these cupcakes is slightly different from other cakes: when inserted, the skewer should come out sticky, with some cake batter on it, to make sure the finished texture is fudgy.

Vegan Chocolate Fudge Cupcakes

FOR THE CUPCAKES
¾ cup soy milk
1 tsp apple cider vinegar
    or lemon juice
1 cup plus 1 Tbsp light
    muscovado sugar
½ cup sunflower oil
1 tsp vanilla extract
1½ cups self-rising flour, sifted
¾ cup cocoa powder
½ tsp baking powder
½ tsp baking soda
¼ tsp salt
¾ cup plus 2 Tbsp coconut
    yogurt

FOR THE CHOCOLATE FROSTING
3 oz good-quality, 70% dairy-
    free dark chocolate, broken
    into pieces, plus 1¾ oz,
    grated (optional), for
    decorating
2 Tbsp coconut cream
7 Tbsp vegetable oil spread
1 tsp vanilla extract
2 cups confectioners' sugar,
    sifted

YOU WILL NEED
12-cup muffin tin, lined
    with 12 paper liners

1 Heat the oven to 400°F.

2 Put the soy milk in a pitcher and add the vinegar or lemon juice. Set aside for 5 minutes to curdle slightly.

3 Whisk together the sugar, oil, and vanilla in a bowl. In a separate large bowl, mix together the flour, cocoa powder, baking powder, baking soda, and salt.

4 Using a balloon whisk, gradually incorporate the soy milk mixture and the sugar mixture into the bowl with the dry ingredients, then add the coconut yogurt and mix until smooth and just incorporated.

5 Spoon the cupcake mixture equally into the paper liners. Bake for 20 minutes, until a skewer inserted into the centers comes out sticky (but not wet). Let cool in the pan for 30 minutes, then transfer to a wire rack to cool completely.

6 To make the frosting, melt the chocolate with the coconut cream in a bowl set over a pot of simmering water. Once the chocolate has melted (3 to 4 minutes), stir to combine, then remove from the heat and let cool slightly.

7 Beat the spread, vanilla, and confectioners' sugar in the bowl of a stand mixer fitted with the paddle attachment, on medium speed for 1 to 2 minutes, until fluffy. Add the chocolate mixture and beat on low speed for 1 minute, until smooth.

8 To decorate, mound buttercream onto the top of each cake. Spread evenly with the swirl of a knife, then finish with a sprinkling of grated dark chocolate, if you wish.

Coconut sugar and naturally sweet carrots and cinnamon, along with a cream cheese and maple topping, give this cake sweetness without the need for refined white sugar.

Naturally Sweet Carrot & Walnut Cake

FOR THE SPONGE
3 large eggs
1¼ cups coconut sugar
½ cup plus 2 Tbsp vegetable oil
1¼ cups all-purpose flour, sifted
1 tsp baking powder
1 tsp ground cinnamon
1 tsp pumpkin pie spice blend
2¾ cups grated carrots
⅓ cup chopped walnuts

FOR THE TOPPING
1 cup plus 2 Tbsp full-fat cream cheese
2 to 3 Tbsp maple syrup
broken-up walnut halves and a few edible flowers, to decorate

YOU WILL NEED
8-inch round, deep cake pan, greased, then lined (base and sides) with parchment paper

1 Heat the oven to 400°F.

2 Make the sponge: Whisk together the eggs, coconut sugar, and vegetable oil in a bowl. In a separate, large bowl, mix together the flour, baking powder, and spices, then stir in the carrots and walnuts until evenly distributed.

3 Add the wet ingredients to the dry and use a wooden spoon to gently combine.

4 Pour the mixture into the prepared pan and bake for 25 to 30 minutes, until a skewer inserted into the center comes out clean. Let cool in the pan for 5 minutes, then turn out onto a wire rack to cool completely.

5 To make the topping, put the cream cheese in a bowl and add 2 tablespoons of the maple syrup. Stir to combine, then taste, and add a little more maple syrup, if needed. Mix until smooth and silky.

6 Level the cooled cake with a bread knife, then transfer it to a cake plate. Using an offset spatula, spread the topping evenly over the cake, making swirls for texture, if you wish.

7 Sprinkle the walnut pieces in a ring around the edge of the topping, and dot with edible flowers for a little color.

A little goes a long way in this intensely delicious and multitextured traybake—it is the perfect accompaniment to a cup of tea or coffee.

Chocolate & Nougat Layer Cake

FOR THE SPONGE
2 tsp instant espresso
½ cup plus 2 Tbsp hot water
1¼ cups gluten-free all-purpose flour, sifted
1 cup granulated sugar
¾ cup plus 3 Tbsp cocoa powder, sifted
2 tsp baking soda
1 tsp baking powder
½ tsp salt
2 extra-large eggs
½ cup plus 2 Tbsp buttermilk
½ cup plus 2 Tbsp vegetable oil
1 Tbsp vanilla extract

FOR THE NOUGAT
¼ cup unsalted butter
1 cup granulated sugar
¼ cup evaporated milk
2½ cups marshmallow cream spread
¼ cup peanut butter
1 tsp vanilla extract
1⅓ cups salted peanuts, roughly chopped

FOR THE CARAMEL
½ cup dulce de leche
sprinkling of flaky sea salt

FOR THE CHOCOLATE
9 oz 54% dark chocolate, finely chopped
½ cup heavy cream
3 Tbsp salted peanuts, roughly chopped

YOU WILL NEED
9 x 13-inch baking pan, greased, then lined (base and sides) with parchment paper

1 Heat the oven to 350°F. Dissolve the espresso powder in the hot water and let cool.

2 For the sponge, beat the flour, sugar, cocoa, baking soda, baking powder, salt, eggs, buttermilk, oil, vanilla, and cooled coffee in the bowl of a stand mixer fitted with the paddle attachment, on medium speed for 2 minutes, until smooth.

3 Pour the mixture into the prepared pan and bake for about 20 minutes, until firm and a skewer inserted into the center comes out clean. Let cool in the pan. (The sponge may be domed at first but it will fall and flatten when cooled.)

4 For the nougat, melt the butter in a medium pot over medium heat. Add the sugar and evaporated milk, stirring until dissolved, then bring to a boil. Reduce the heat and simmer for 5 minutes, stirring occasionally, until golden brown. Remove the pot from the heat and pour the mixture into the bowl of a stand mixer fitted with the paddle attachment. Let cool for 5 minutes.

5 Add the marshmallow cream spread, peanut butter, and vanilla extract to the bowl and beat on low speed for 1 minute, until well combined, then fold in the peanuts.

6 Spread the dulce de leche over the cooled sponge and sprinkle lightly with sea salt. Pour the warm nougat over the cake and smooth with an offset spatula. Allow to set for 1 hour.

7 For the chocolate layer, place the chopped chocolate in a bowl. Pour the cream into a small pot and place over medium heat. As soon as it comes to a boil, pour it over the chocolate and let stand for 1 minute, then stir until smooth. Allow to cool slightly, then pour the mixture over the nougat layer and sprinkle with the chopped peanuts. Chill for 2 to 3 hours, until set, then turn out and cut into 24 slices.

You can make this cake more or less marbled simply by swirling the batters together with a skewer—the more you swirl, the more patterns you'll create.

Vegan Marble Cake

1¼ cups soy milk
1 Tbsp apple cider vinegar
or lemon juice
1 cup plus 2 Tbsp granulated
sugar
¾ cup plus 2 Tbsp vegetable oil
spread
2 tsp vanilla extract
2¾ cups plus 2 Tbsp self-rising
flour, sifted
1 tsp baking powder
3 Tbsp cocoa powder

YOU WILL NEED
2 medium disposable
piping bags
9-inch Bundt pan, greased

1 Heat the oven to 400°F.

2 Put the soy milk in a pitcher and stir in the vinegar or lemon juice. Set aside for 5 minutes to curdle slightly.

3 Beat the sugar, spread, and vanilla in the bowl of a stand mixer fitted with the paddle attachment, on high speed for 2 to 3 minutes, until pale and creamy.

4 With the mixer on low speed, gradually add the curdled soy milk and beat for 30 to 60 seconds. Add the flour and baking powder, and mix on low until just incorporated.

5 Spoon one third of the mixture into a separate bowl and stir in the cocoa powder. Then spoon the chocolate mixture into a medium piping bag.

6 Spoon the vanilla mixture into a separate piping bag, snip a ¾-inch opening in the end, and pipe one third into the greased Bundt pan, in a random pattern.

7 Snip the end of the piping bag containing the chocolate mixture and randomly dot blobs of chocolate in and around the vanilla. Then switch back—alternating bag by bag until you have used up both mixtures.

8 To marble the sponge, drag a skewer through the mixtures in a wavy motion all around the pan, so you can see streaks.

9 Bake the sponge for 25 minutes, until a skewer inserted into the center comes out clean. Allow to cool in the pan for 5 to 10 minutes, then turn out onto a wire rack to cool completely.

Kim-Joy's vegan celebration cake from Season 9 requires a bit of skill, but it is sure to impress. If you don't have time for the whole creation, try making just the cookies to enjoy with a cup of tea.

Vegan Lavender & Lemon Fox Cake

Kim-Joy

FOR THE 9-INCH BASE TIER
5⅔ cups self-rising cake flour, sifted
2 cups granulated sugar
5 tsp edible dried lavender
2¼ tsp baking powder
1 tsp salt
2⅔ cups soy milk
1 cup sunflower oil
5 tsp aquafaba (see page 237)
2½ tsp white wine vinegar

FOR THE 7-INCH TOP TIER
3⅔ cups self-rising cake flour, sifted
1¼ cups granulated sugar
1½ tsp baking powder
¾ tsp salt
2 tsp edible dried lavender
1⅔ cups soy milk
½ cup plus 2 Tbsp sunflower oil
4½ tsp aquafaba
1 Tbsp white wine vinegar

FOR THE VEGAN LEMON CURD
⅓ cup cornstarch
½ cup lemon-infused sugar
juice of 5 lemons
5 Tbsp soy milk
6 Tbsp extra-virgin coconut oil

FOR THE VEGAN COOKIES
1¼ cups all-purpose flour, sifted
a pinch of salt
2 Tbsp granulated sugar
½ tsp vanilla extract
6 Tbsp coconut oil

1 Heat the oven to 350°F. Make the sponge for the bottom tier: Mix all the dry ingredients together in a large bowl and whisk all the wet ingredients together in another large bowl. Add the dry ingredients to the wet, and whisk until smooth and just combined.

2 Pour the mixture equally into the three larger pans and bake for 15 to 20 minutes, until a skewer inserted in the centers comes out clean. Immediately turn out the sponges onto a wire rack and peel off the parchment paper. Let cool.

3 Mix together the sponge ingredients for the smaller, top-tier cakes, as before, and bake for 15 to 20 minutes, until a skewer inserted into the centers comes out clean. Turn out onto a wire rack and let cool.

4 Meanwhile, make the lemon curd: Whisk together the cornstarch and 7 tablespoons of water to a smooth paste. Place in a small pot and stir in the sugar and lemon juice.

5 Cook over medium heat, stirring occasionally, until all the sugar has dissolved, then keep stirring until the mixture has thickened and you can no longer taste the cornstarch.

6 Turn the heat down to low and add the soy milk and coconut oil. Stir briskly until the oil has melted and the mixture is smooth, then pour into the shallow bowl, cover with plastic wrap, and freeze for about 45 minutes.

7 Make the cookies: Combine all the dry ingredients and vanilla in a bowl, then rub in the coconut oil. Add 2 tablespoons of water and shape into a dough ball.

8 Roll out the dough on a floured work surface to about ¼ inch thick. Cut out three mushroom shapes and three fox

ingredients and recipe continue

FOR THE ROYAL ICING
7 Tbsp aquafaba
4 cups confectioners' sugar,
    sifted
orange food-coloring
    paste or gel
honey-gold food-coloring
    paste or gel
brown food-coloring
    paste or gel
½ tsp cocoa powder

FOR THE VEGAN BUTTERCREAM
¾ cup plus 2 Tbsp vegetable oil
    spread, diced
2 cups vegetable shortening
4 cups confectioners' sugar,
    sifted
pink food-coloring
    paste or gel
dark green food-coloring paste
    or gel
light green food-coloring paste
    or gel
lime green food-coloring
    paste or gel

YOU WILL NEED
9-inch round, deep cake pans x
    3, greased, then base-lined
    with parchment paper
7-inch round, deep cake pans x
    3, greased, then base-lined
    with parchment paper
shallow bowl
baking sheet lined with
    parchment paper
6 small disposable piping bags
large disposable piping bag
10-inch round, thin cake board
8-inch round, thin cake board
cake-decorating turntable
tall cake smoother
4 dowels
large piping bag fitted with
    a medium closed star nozzle
large piping bag fitted with
    a small petal nozzle

shapes. Place on the lined baking sheet and bake for 8 to 10 minutes, until slightly browned at the edges. Transfer to a wire rack to cool.

9 Meanwhile, make the royal icing: Beat 5 tablespoons of the aquafaba in the bowl of a stand mixer fitted with the paddle attachment, on medium-high speed until frothy, then add half the confectioners' sugar and mix on medium-low speed until smooth.

10 Add the remaining confectioners' sugar and mix until the icing leaves a ribbon trail when you lift the beater. Add more confectioners' sugar if the mixture is too runny.

11 Spoon about two thirds of the royal icing into a medium bowl, then divide this into three unequal portions—you'll need slightly more of one portion than the other two.

12 Color the larger portion with orange coloring and a tiny amount of the honey-gold to make an orange with a tinge of golden brown. Add the brown coloring and cocoa powder to one of the smaller portions for a deep brown color. Leave the remaining portion white.

13 Divide the icing colors into the small piping bags as follows, and set aside:
» Orange: ¼ into 1 piping bag and ¾ into another.
» Brown: all into 1 piping bag.
» White: ¼ into 1 piping bag and ¾ into another.

14 Add enough orange coloring to give a bright orange color to the remaining icing in the mixer bowl, and stir in 1 tablespoon of aquafaba at a time, until the icing is runny enough for a controlled drip on the side of a cake pan. Cover with plastic wrap and set aside.

15 Make the buttercream: Put the spread into the clean bowl of the bowl of a stand mixer fitted with the paddle attachment and mix on medium-low speed until smooth. Mix in the vegetable shortening until smooth and combined.

16 Mix in one third of the confectioners' sugar until combined, then add the remaining confectioners' sugar, gradually increasing the speed each time, until the buttercream is white and smooth. Put half the buttercream into the large disposable piping bag. Divide and color the remainder as follows, and set aside:

» About ⅔ cup buttercream colored pink.

» About ⅔ cup buttercream colored dark green.

» About 2 tablespoons of buttercream colored light green. Leave the remainder in the bowl.

17 Assemble the base: Place the larger cake board on the turntable. Snip a large tip on the piping bag of white buttercream and pipe a blob on the cake board. Top with a large sponge.

18 Spread a little buttercream from the bowl over the surface of the cake and, from the piping bag, pipe a white buttercream "dam" around the top edge of the cake (this is to prevent the lemon curd from seeping out). Spoon 2 to 3 tablespoons of the lemon curd on top and spread evenly. Repeat with a second large sponge and then top with the third large sponge.

19 Spread the white buttercream from the bowl on top of the cake and around the sides. Spread a few smears of pink buttercream here and there on the sides. Smooth the top, then the sides using the cake smoother. Aim for a thin crumb coat. Insert the dowels into the cake and transfer to the fridge.

20 Assemble the top tier. Place the smaller cake board onto the turntable and stack and frost the smaller sponge layers just as you did for the base tier, except this time using dark green buttercream on the top and a combination of white and dark green buttercream on the sides.

21 Mark the outline of a fox shape on the top of the uppermost cake using a toothpick.

22 Snip a very small hole in the piping bag containing the smaller amount of orange royal icing, and snip a small–medium tip on the bag containing the larger amount of orange royal icing. Repeat for the white royal icing. Snip a small tip on the brown royal icing.

recipe continues

23 Use the small-tipped piping bags of orange and white royal icing to pipe the outline of the fox. Use the larger tipped bags to "flood" the orange and white areas. Working quickly, use the toothpick to blend the white and orange by the tip of the tail. Allow to set, then add the legs, nose, and mouth.

24 Meanwhile, start piping the cookies, piping the foxes in exactly the way you did for the cake. Pipe orange over the mushroom cookies (outline first, then flooding), and pipe on white dots while the orange icing is still wet.

25 Remove the first cake tier from the fridge and place the second tier on top. Using a large spoon, pour the thinned orange icing in carefully controlled drips down the side of the bottom cake tier.

26 To make the roses and swirls, marble the pink buttercream with a little of the remaining white buttercream, but don't over-mix, then divide it in half and place each half in a large piping bag—one fitted with the closed star nozzle and the other with the petal nozzle. Pipe swirls around the base of each tier and pipe roses on top.

27 Color any remaining white buttercream with lime green and place this in the remaining small piping bag. Snip the end into a V shape and pipe tiny green leaves between the roses.

28 Decorate the cake with the fox and mushroom cookies.

Aquafaba creates a less stable meringue than egg white, so it's best to make the layers for this stack in advance, then assemble just before serving.

Strawberries & "Cream" Vegan Meringue Cake

1⅔ cups aquafaba
   (see page 237)
1 tsp cream of tartar
2⅔ cups granulated sugar
seeds of 1 vanilla pod
2 tsp xanthan gum
½ cup plus 1 Tbsp vegan white
   chocolate chips, melted

FOR THE COCONUT CREAM
3 x 13.5 oz cans of good-
   quality coconut milk,
   refrigerated overnight
2 tsp vanilla extract

TO DECORATE
4½ cups strawberries, hulled
   and sliced (reserve a few
   whole and halved fruits
   for decoration)

YOU WILL NEED
4 baking sheets, greased,
   then lined with parchment
   paper
large piping bag fitted with
   a large closed star nozzle
large cake-decorating
   paintbrush

1 Heat the oven to 250°F. Draw an 8-inch circle on each sheet of parchment paper lining the sheets, and turn the paper upside down so that the marking is on the underside.

2 To make the meringue, pour the aquafaba into the bowl of a stand mixer fitted with the whisk attachment. Add the cream of tartar and whisk on medium speed for 3 to 5 minutes, until foamy. Increase the speed to high and whisk for 5 to 10 minutes to stiff peaks.

3 Add the sugar, 1 tablespoon at a time, whisking after each addition to a stiff meringue. Add the vanilla seeds and sift the xanthan gum over the meringue. Whisk for another 30 seconds.

4 Spoon the mixture into the large piping bag fitted with a star nozzle and pipe four disks of meringue with a decorative edge, using the circles you've drawn on the paper as guides, onto the baking sheets.

5 Bake the meringue disks for 2½ hours, until crisp and firm (they may still feel a little soft underneath). Remove from the oven and let cool on the baking sheets.

6 Carefully turn over each disk and peel off the parchment paper, leaving the meringues' undersides facing upward.

7 Melt the chocolate in a bowl set over a pot of gently simmering water, then gently paint the chocolate over the base of each meringue and allow the chocolate to set.

8 To make the coconut cream, spoon out the layer of solid coconut milk at the top of each chilled can into a bowl (taking care not to add any of the watery liquid at this stage). Add

recipe continues

the vanilla and whisk with an electric hand mixer until smooth, adding 1 to 2 tablespoons of the coconut water to loosen, if necessary.

9 To assemble the cake, place the first disk on a cake plate. Neatly spread one quarter of the coconut cream over the meringue, all the way to the edge. Place strawberry slices around the edge in a neat ring. Fill the middle of the ring with a layer of strawberries to cover the cream, using about one third of the strawberries total.

10 Place another meringue disk on top and repeat the process of spreading cream and placing strawberry slices as in Step 9. Repeat for another layer, then top with the last meringue disk. Spread the remaining coconut cream on top and decorate the top of the cake with the reserved whole and halved strawberries. Serve immediately.

This is a quick-to-make and very pretty crowd-pleaser of a traybake—serve it with ice cream for an after-supper treat or enjoy it just as it is.

Gluten-Free Cherry & Pistachio Traybake

1½ cups unsalted butter,
   softened
1¼ cups plus 2 Tbsp
   granulated sugar
6 large eggs
1 cup plus 3 Tbsp gluten-free
   all-purpose flour, sifted
4 tsp baking powder
¼ tsp salt
2 cups ground pistachios
7 oz cherries, halved and pitted

YOU WILL NEED
9 x 13-inch baking pan,
   greased, then lined
   (base and sides)
   with parchment paper

1 Heat the oven to 400°F.

2 Beat the butter and sugar in the bowl of a stand mixer fitted with the paddle attachment, on medium speed for 1 to 2 minutes, until pale and creamy.

3 With the mixer on low speed, add the eggs, one at a time, beating well after each addition.

4 In a separate bowl, mix the flour, baking powder, salt, and ground pistachios together.

5 Using a metal spoon, fold the dry mixture into the wet mixture until incorporated.

6 Carefully fold the cherries into the mixture until evenly distributed, then pour the batter into the prepared pan.

7 Bake the sponge for 25 to 30 minutes, until golden brown and a skewer inserted into the center comes out clean. Let cool completely in the pan, then cut into 16 equal pieces.

SERVES **12** HANDS-ON **25** MINS BAKE **30** MINS

We have chosen raspberries and raspberry jam for the topping and filling of this vegan version of the much-loved Victoria sponge, but rustic blackberry or classic strawberry is also delicious.

Vegan Victoria Sponge

FOR THE SPONGE
1¼ cups soy milk
1 Tbsp apple cider vinegar
 or lemon juice
1 cup plus 2 Tbsp granulated
 sugar
¾ cup plus 2 Tbsp vegetable oil
 spread
2 tsp vanilla extract
2¾ cups plus 2 Tbsp self-rising
 flour, sifted
1 tsp baking powder

**FOR THE FILLING
& DECORATION**
6 Tbsp vegetable oil spread
1¼ cups confectioners' sugar,
 plus extra for dusting
1 Tbsp vanilla extract
2 Tbsp soy milk
½ cup homemade or good-
 quality raspberry jam
a handful of raspberries,
 to decorate

YOU WILL NEED
8-inch round cake pans x 2,
 greased, then lined
 (base and sides)
 with parchment paper

1 Heat the oven to 400°F.

2 Put the soy milk in a pitcher and add the vinegar or lime juice. Let rest for 5 minutes, to curdle slightly.

3 Beat the sugar, spread, and vanilla in the bowl of a stand mixer fitted with the paddle attachment, on medium-high speed for 5 minutes, until pale and creamy.

4 With the mixer on low speed, gradually add the curdled soy milk, beating for 1 minute, until combined. Add the flour and baking powder, and mix on low until just incorporated.

5 Divide the cake mixture equally between the prepared pans and bake for 25 to 30 minutes, until a skewer inserted into the centers comes out clean. Allow the cakes to cool in the pans for 5 minutes, then turn out onto a wire rack to cool completely.

6 While the cakes are cooling, make the filling: Put the spread, confectioners' sugar, and vanilla in the bowl of a stand mixer fitted with the paddle attachment and beat on low speed for 2 to 3 minutes, until fluffy. Beat in the soy milk, a little at a time, to loosen the mixture (you may not need all the soy milk).

7 To assemble, place one of the cooled sponges top-side downward on a cake plate. Spread the jam over the cake, then spoon the filling over the jam, spreading it evenly to the edges.

8 Place the second cake, top-side upward, on top of the filling. Dust with confectioners' sugar, then top with raspberries, to decorate.

CONVERSION TABLE

US CUP

INGREDIENTS	1 CUP	¾ CUP	⅔ CUP	½ CUP	⅓ CUP	¼ CUP	2 TBSP
All-purpose flour	125g	95g	85g	60g	40g	30g	15g
Brown sugar	215g	160g	140g	105g	70g	55g	25g
Butter	225g	170g	150g	115g	75g	55g	30g
Confectioners' sugar	125g	95g	85g	60g	40g	30g	15g
Cornstarch	110g	85g	75g	55g	40g	30g	15g
Granulated sugar	200g	150g	130g	100g	65g	50g	25g
Hazelnuts (chopped)	175g	130g	115g	90g	60g	45g	20g
Hazelnuts (ground)	110g	85g	75g	55g	40g	30g	15g
Raisins	145g	110g	95g	75g	50g	35g	20g
Raspberries	120g	90g	80g	60g	40g	30g	15g
Rolled oats	90g	70g	60g	45g	30g	25g	10g
Salt	300g	225g	200g	150g	100g	75g	40g
Water/milk	240ml	180ml	160ml	120ml	80ml	60ml	30ml

COOK'S NOTES

Oven temperatures: Ovens vary—not only from brand to brand, but from the front to the back of the oven, as well as between the top and bottom shelves. Get to know your oven, and where its hot spots are, and invest in an oven thermometer if you can. Always preheat the oven, and use dry oven mitts.

Eggs: Eggs should be at room temperature for baking cakes unless specified. Some recipes may contain raw or partially cooked eggs. Pregnant women, the elderly, babies and toddlers, and people who are unwell should be aware of these recipes.

Herbs and fruit: Use fresh herbs and fresh, medium-sized fruit unless the recipe specifies otherwise.

Salt: If you're using sea salt, it is best to crush the flakes into a fine powder before measuring and adding to your recipe (unless sea salt is specified).

Spoon measures: All teaspoons and tablespoons are level unless otherwise stated.

INDEX

Published in the United States by Clarkson Potter/Publishers,
an imprint of Random House, a division of Penguin Random House
LLC, New York. Originally published in hardcover in Great Britain as
The Great British Bake Off: The Big Book of Amazing Cakes by
Sphere, an imprint of Little, Brown Book Group, a division of
Hachette UK, London, in 2019.
clarksonpotter.com

CLARKSON POTTER is a trademark and POTTER with
colophon is a registered trademark of Penguin Random House LLC.

Library of Congress Cataloging-in-Publication Data

Title: The Great British baking show : the big book of amazing cakes.
Description: New York : Clarkson Potter, 2019. | Includes index.
Identifiers: LCCN 2019035491 (print) | LCCN 2019035492 (ebook) |
ISBN 9780593138397 (hardcover) | ISBN 9780593138403 (ebook)
Subjects: LCSH: Great British bake off. | Cake. | Baking—Great
Britain.
Classification: LCC TX771.C558 2020 (print) | LCC TX771 (ebook) |
DDC 641.86/53—dc23
LC record available at https://lccn.loc.gov/2019035491.
LC ebook record available at https://lccn.loc.gov/2019035492.

ISBN 978-0-593-13839-7
Ebook ISBN 978-0-593-13840-3

Printed in China

10 9 8 7 6 5 4 3 2

First American Edition

PICTURE CREDITS

Every effort has been made to trace and acknowledge copyright
holders. Any errors or omissions are unintentional and we will, if
informed, make necessary corrections in future editions of this book.
Garden Photo Library: p. 65 (bottom left) Derek St Romaine/
GardenPhotoLibrary; Getty Images: pp. 249 Geography Photos/
Universal Images Group, 271 Tim Graham; and Shutterstock:
pp. 4–5 Alik Mulikov, 73–4 Matt Gibson, 213 Matthew J Thomas,
229 Kirsty Matt.

WITH THANKS

Love Productions would like to thank the following people:
Producer: Chloë Avery
Challenge Producer: Tallulah Radula-Scott
Food Team: Katy Bigley, Georgia Harding, Emma Hair
Home Economist: Becca Watson
Love Executives: Letty Kavanagh, Rupert Frisby, Kieran Smith, Anna Beattie
Publicists: Amanda Console and Shelagh Pymm
Commissioning Editors: Kelly Webb-Lamb, Sarah Lazenby

Thank you to Paul, Prue, Noel and Sandi. And to the bakers for their recipes: Alice, Amelia, Dan,
David, Helena, Henry, Jamie, Michael, Michelle, Phil, Priya, Rosie and Steph, Andrew, Beca, Briony,
Edd, Flora, Frances, Jo, John, Kim-Joy, Liam, Mary-Anne, Miranda, Nancy, Rahul, Rob, Selasi,
Sophie, and all the bakers from the last ten years.